The Labour Movement in Britain

A Commentary

JOHN SAVILLE

faber and faber

LONDON · BOSTON

First published in 1988
by Faber and Faber Limited
3 Queen Square London WC1N 3AU

Printed in Great Britain by Mackays of Chatham Kent

British Library Cataloguing in Publication Data
Saville, John
The labour movement in Britain.—
(Historical handbook series).
1. labor and laboring classes—Great
Britain—History—20th century
2. Socialism—Great Britain—History—
20th century
I. Title   II. Series
335'.1'0941   HD8390

ISBN 0-571-14975-8

The Labour Movement in Britain

Historical Handbooks

Series Editors:
Avner Offer – University of York
F. M. L. Thompson – Institute of Historical Research,
University of London

It is widely recognized that many of the problems of present-day society are deeply rooted in the past, but the actual lines of historical development are often known only to a few specialists, while the policy-makers and analysts themselves frequently rely on a simplified, dramatized, and misleading version of history. Just as the urban landscape of today was largely built in a world that is no longer familiar, so the policy landscape is shaped by attitudes and institutions formed under very different conditions in the past. This series of specially commissioned handbooks aims to provide short, up-to-date studies in the evolution of current problems, not in the form of narratives but as critical accounts of the ways in which the present is formed by the past, and of the roots of present discontents. Designed for those with little time for extensive reading in the specialized literature, the books contain full bibliographies for further study. The authors aim to be as accurate and comprehensive as possible, but not anodyne; their arguments, forcefully expressed, make the historical experience available in challenging form, but do not presume to offer ready-made solutions.

To the family Miliband
with love

Contents

Acknowledgements

The arguments in this book have been discussed with divers friends and (intellectual) enemies over many years, and I am grateful and appreciative of many private conversations and public debates.

I have to thank the Leverhulme Trustees for their generosity in awarding me, soon after my formal retirement, an Emeritus Fellowship for research into aspects of twentieth-century politics.

Finally, let me put on record my considerable indebtedness to the editors of this series for the care with which they read my manuscript, and for the perceptive comments they suggested. Professor F. M. L. Thompson and Dr Avner Offer do not share my own political approach to the matters discussed, and I can only acknowledge their generous acceptance of a text some parts of which, at least, they must have felt misguided.

JOHN SAVILLE
August 1987

1
Introduction

The Labour Party in 1951, after being in power for just over six years, obtained the highest vote ever recorded in a British general election, although it failed on this occasion to win a parliamentary majority. Its vote was nearly 14 million, representing just under 50 per cent of the total votes cast. By 1974, when it was to become the Government, the Labour Party polled 2.5 million votes less than in 1951, and in 1983, at the lowest point of its electoral history in the postwar years, the votes it received were around 8.5 million, some 27.6 per cent of the total. In the general election of 1987 there was little change; Labour's vote was up by just over 3 per cent and its share of the total rose to 30.8 per cent.

Between the 1940s and the 1980s, then, Labour lost dramatically the votes of many of the social groups in the population which had supported it in the immediate postwar years; and the trends were well established before the first Thatcher Government came to power in 1979. What is generally agreed among electoral analysts is that the decline had already begun by the time of the general election of 1955, and that while election results emphatically do not tell the whole story of political attitudes within a society, they are a broad guide of an approximate kind. Labour, it would seem, has lost certain of the middle-class groups which voted for some degree of radical change in the 1940s, but more significant, the last quarter of a century has seen the move away from Labour of important sections of its working-class constituency. The Labour Party was never at any time in its history the sole party of the working class, for the Tories, going well back in the nineteenth century, have always had a quite substantial working-class vote; but there is no doubt that the Labour Party, from its establishment in 1900, began to attract to itself an increasing proportion of the working-class electorate, including the largest part of the trade union vote. By the 1980s Labour had retained the support of the more traditional working class of the council estates, the industrial areas of the North and, in general, the workers in the traditional industries of the nineteenth century. In Scotland, in 1987, the Tories were reduced to a handful of seats, and in Wales Labour remained powerful; but now it was the skilled workers of the South and the Midlands who voted in critical numbers for the Tories and who continued to reject Labour in the elections of 1983 and 1987. The ethnic vote has nearly always gone to Labour, but there may well be changes of allegiance in the future.

These are the simplified but stark electoral facts to which the chapters that follow offer an historical background. They do not provide or prescribe a solution. What is attempted is to propose some of the reasons for the emergence of the particular variety of British Labour socialism in the first half of the twentieth century, and to offer suggestions for the decline in support of the Labour Party in the most recent period of our history. It may be helpful to discuss briefly some general questions of political history before moving into the chronological narrative.

It is necessary to distinguish between parties of social reform which, regardless of their social base, work for social reform within the existing framework of society and reformist socialist parties. Of the former, the Liberal Party was certainly a party of social reform, and while the Conservative Party was responsible for a number of important legislative changes, it was the Liberals in the later nineteenth century who affixed to themselves the title of 'The Party of Progress'. By contrast, European societies of the twentieth century have seen the emergence of reformist socialist parties whose long-term objectives have been the transformation of capitalism into one or other version of socialism, to be accomplished through the abolition of private property in the means of production, but always by parliamentary means and through the modification of existing institutions. The twentieth century has also seen the growth of revolutionary or quasi-revolutionary movements and organizations: syndicalism, anarchism and political parties owing allegiance to some form of Marxism. After the 1917 Russian Revolution most revolutionary energy was concentrated in Communist Parties. In Britain the Communist Party was always a minority trend, more important in certain periods than in others, but it is the Labour Party which overwhelmingly has been the expression of working-class aspirations. To be specific, the British Labour Party may be characterized as a party of social reform with a reformist socialist left wing whose political and intellectual arguments have often been taken over in general statements of policy by the Labour Party as a whole. Since 1918 the Labour Party has formally been committed to a socialist programme with the adoption of the famous clause four, which reads:

> To secure for the producers by hand or brain the full fruits of their industry, and the most equitable distribution thereof that may be possible, upon the basis of the common ownership of the means of production and the best obtainable system of popular administration and control of each industry and service.

The political and social practice of labourism has been concerned – often passionately concerned – with the remedying of poverty and social injustice; and the most important achievement of British Labour in the twentieth century has been the progressive incorporation of social welfare policies into public politics. It must be remarked that such has been the political density, power and solidarity of the propertied classes in Britain that social reform of any significance has come only after bitter and long-fought political struggles; and the rancour of those struggles has led many within the Labour Party, and most outside, to endow what has been achieved with much greater significance than has often been the case. Social welfare measures in Britain have come, therefore, to be identified in many minds with socialism.

To foreign observers one of the most surprising aspects of British politics has been the length of time it has taken Labour to win an overall parliamentary majority at Westminster. The party was established in 1900; and it took a world war of gross butchery, a persistently high level of unemployment during the two decades which followed, with many areas of material poverty, and a Second World War of six years' duration before the Labour Party won an unassailable majority in the summer of 1945; a remarkable demonstration of the conservatism of British society. But in those years immediately following the end of the Second World War there was a feeling for change and a willingness to accept change; a firm rejection of the unemployment and the poverty of the pre-1939 years; and a determination never again to allow those conditions to return. The radicalism which produced these sentiments may have been diffuse and unfocused, but it was earnest and authentic, and it lasted more or less through the next two decades, encouraging a consensus on social questions between the main political parties. It was, however, a consensus whose intellectual and political foundations were slowly eroding, and the Labour Party and the trade unions proved incapable of developing a future policy that was progressive: one that offered a serious challenge to the existing order in the interests of the majority. Their failure was reflected in the declining loss of support at the polls, culminating in the Tory victory of 1979 and what could well be over a decade of Thatcher administrations.

It is often argued that a reforming party always loses support with an improvement in living standards and general affluence. It is an argument with a long history in Britain, going back at least as far as the Chartists, and up to the present it takes in, as one version, the Leninist theory of the labour aristocracy. It also used to be believed that the converse was true; namely, that impoverishment would produce radicalization. The Communist International asserted this thesis in the crisis of 1929. Both sides of the argument have a point to them and examples can certainly be offered in support of either side. What can, however, be said for Britain as for elsewhere is that it has not generally been the worst off materially who have provided the radical/revolutionary energy for mass agitations, and there is, further, no necessary correlation between relative affluence and a weakening of radical attitudes. The matter is a complex one, and each social group, in the determination of political and social ideas and attitudes, involves a subtle and multiple analysis.

It is, of course, true that in a country with such strong conservative traditions as Britain, the persistence of radical opinions requires constant debate and discussion; and the intervention of human agency, individually and collectively, is always necessary. Without a continuous renewal of the argument for progressive change – and argument in this context means all and every aspect of political activity accepted in a political democracy – there will be no alteration in the existing power structures and institutions; and government of the people by the people and for the people become words with less and less meaning. It is the argument of this book that the Labour Party and its associated organizations have failed in the most recent decades to encourage the hopes and widen the aspirations of a majority of the British people who could reasonably be expected to provide their constituency; and it is this failure which has produced the sobering electoral statistics set forth above.

In historical terms the Labour Party has performed two roles in British politics; on the one hand it has been, directly or indirectly, the main agent of social change during the twentieth century, and the greater part of the idealism and personal self-sacrifice generated within British society has found expression in the broad Labour movement. Without that, Britain would be a less civilized society today. On the other hand, the leadership of the Labour movement, again in all its parts, has been the main agent of social control, in that it has been central to the maintenance of the social stability which has been a remarkable feature of British society in the decades of imperial decline against the background of an exceedingly tumultuous and crisis-ridden world situation. These two roles, the encouragement of social change and the preservation of the basic structures of society, are integrally related and their understanding requires a sophisticated and complicated analysis that cannot be subsumed under simple and schematic headings. What follows here is no more than the beginnings of an interpretation.

2
The nineteenth-century background

Britain had a unique social formation during the nineteenth century. The near-complete elimination of the peasantry from the countryside before modern industrialization got under way at the end of the eighteenth century meant that the overwhelming majority of the population, in both country and town, were wage-labourers. The virtual absence of a peasantry in Britain produced a social structure quite different from all other industrializing societies in Europe, and the fact of proletarianization gave British society certain special characteristics much earlier than anywhere else in the world. Industrialization also meant urbanization. The most rapid growth of the large towns took place in the first half of the nineteenth century, and by 1851 the population census for England and Wales recorded half the population living in urban areas. The century that followed saw the processes of centralization continue. By the 1950s two-fifths of the British people lived in seven major conurbations, and almost one-fifth in the largest of all, the metropolitan area of London.

The early development of manufacturing production, mostly as domestic industry, encouraged the growth of collectivist sentiment and action among the manual workers, and especially among those who were artisans. Throughout the eighteenth century combinations of skilled workers, as well as some who were unskilled, developed among many trades and in many areas. London, the centre of the artisan trades in the eighteenth century, together with the rapidly growing textile districts, provided the largest number of trade combinations and recorded disputes. Organization of workers was not necessarily permanent, but against the background of rapidly extending industrial change the potential for collective action was steadily accumulating. Trade combinations almost always included the social benefits of friendly societies – indeed this is how many had started – and in the half century before the Reform Bill of 1832 the growth of trade combinations, and the sense of solidarity which combination encouraged, led to the emergence of radical politics among working people. There developed a sentiment of class that found expression in increasingly sophisticated critiques of contemporary society. This massive weighting of manual workers in British society has been the starting point for any analysis of social politics from the late eighteenth century on. There was nowhere else in Europe in the nineteenth century where universal suffrage would have given proletarians a numerical majority. The mass movement of Chartism before 1850 turned upon this understanding, and given that before 1848 political democracy carried economic and social implications, it is not difficult to appreciate the implacable hostility to an extension of the suffrage on the part of the propertied classes.[1] The Whig historian, Macaulay, provided a statement of their fears and anxieties in the debate in the House of Commons on the presentation of the Second Chartist Petition in 1842:

But I believe that universal suffrage would be fatal to all purposes for which government exists, and for which aristocracies and all other things exist, and that it is utterly incompatible with the very existence of civilisation. I conceive that civilisation rests on the security of property . . . and if it be the fact, that all classes have the deepest interest in the security of property, I conceive, that this principle follows, that we never can, without absolute danger, entrust the supreme Government of the country to any class which would, to a moral certainty, be induced to commit great and systematic inroads against the security of property.

The Chartist movement, the first mass movement of working people in the history of industrial capitalism, was largely destroyed, physically and politically, by 1848. Its more or less complete demise was accomplished over the next half-dozen years, the result of a judicious combination of force and guile on the part of the ruling classes, and the conflicts and tensions within the radical movement itself. Thereafter, in the second half of the nineteenth century, no independent party existed which represented the interests of working people, an historical paradox in the most proletarian country in the world that is of the first importance for the analysis of modern British history. The density and solidity of the economic and social structures of British society after 1850, with increasing industrial growth, rapidly extending overseas trade and an expanding Empire, provided the basis for a political stability that was in marked contrast with the first half of the century. There was a confidence infused with arrogance among the propertied groups when they looked upon the masses of their own people and reflected upon their own power; although their more intelligent representatives always remembered, as Gladstone phrased it in a private letter of April 1865, 'that we have got to govern millions of hard hands; that it must be done by force, fraud, or goodwill; that the latter has been tried and is answering'. It was much in the recollection of the leading politicians that the 'millions of hard hands' had been exceedingly troublesome through the first half of the century, and that the coercive powers of the state had been widely used. But now it was different, and it was becoming generally appreciated that political democracy would sooner or later have to be extended to the millions of the propertyless. When Palmerston died in 1865 the extension of the franchise to some additional groups could not be indefinitely delayed. The problems were, first, how to limit the effectiveness of such an extension in electoral terms, and then how to curb and contain its political consequences. Walter Bagehot offered the classic text for the taming of the political democracy that was slowly coming into existence. In the introduction to the second edition of *The English Constitution*, published in 1872 after the Second Reform Act had given the vote to some groups of working men in the towns, Bagehot proffered a forceful exposition of the matter to the politicians on the new period they were entering: 'They have to guide the new voters in the exercise of the franchise; to guide them quietly, and without saying what they are doing, but still to guide them.' The politicians, Bagehot continued, have to set out the political questions for national discussion. If these political questions are wrongly presented, or fail to evoke a positive response, then it could come about that the working classes might be alienated to the point where they developed an independent movement or organization 'as a class together'. And that would be a disaster:

> But in all cases it must be remembered that a political combination of the lower classes, as such and for their own objects, is an evil of the first magnitude; that a permanent combination of them would make them (now that so many of them have the suffrage) supreme in the country; and that their supremacy, in the state they now are, means the supremacy of ignorance over instruction and of numbers over knowledge.

Bagehot offered the way out, although he appreciated that his advice, in any given circumstances, might well go against 'the combative propensities of man', by which he meant vested interests of all kinds. But what had to be avoided was an unbending intransigence on the part of the owners of property and wealth, and politicians, confronted with the democratic majority, had a clear obligation not to encourage the lower orders to resist, and thereby to learn how to fight:

> So long as they are not taught to act together, there is a chance of this being averted, and it can only be averted by the greatest wisdom and the greatest foresight in the higher classes. They must avoid, not only every evil, but

every appearance of evil; while they have still the power they must remove, not only every actual grievance, but, where it is possible, every seeming grievance too; they must willingly concede every claim which they can safely concede, in order that they may not have to concede unwillingly some claim which would impair the safety of the country.

What became clear in the decades which followed the Second Reform Act was the moderation of the demands coming from below. It was Ireland and the Irish question that proved so much more difficult than the issues of domestic politics. Political moderation in Britain was encouraged by many influences. One was the restriction of the working-class franchise by the vagaries of the electoral registration system. In the last two general elections before the First World War it has been estimated that only about 60 per cent of adult males were technically able to vote; and almost all those excluded would be working-class voters. The proportion voting was always low before 1914, due not least to the difficulties of registration experienced by working-class voters; and these institutional obstructions undoubtedly contributed to the general conservatism of the British political system.[2] But even with reforming governments there were many obstacles in the way of progressive legislation, with the House of Lords always acting as a severe brake upon social change. An early example of the political dilatoriness which the British parliamentary system encouraged at all points was the length of time it took to put old age pensions on to the statute book. The issue was first raised in the late 1870s; and it took several Select Committees, one Royal Commission, and thirty years until the first measure was accepted in 1908. It is true that in this matter as in many social innovations – children's allowances in the interwar years was another – working-class organizations were also opposed to change; in the case of old age pensions, it was certain of the skilled trade unions and the friendly societies until about the turn of the century; but whatever the combination of reasons, delay and procrastination were built into the British structure of government. As the future Lord Salisbury commented in 1861 – the occasion was a Church Rates Abolition Bill: 'There was left to them the chances of war, and it might be victory, but at any rate they had obtained delay, and delay was life.' For the propertied classes, delay was always life. When Hyndman went to see Disraeli just before the latter died in 1881, Disraeli tried to explain how powerful the forces of conservatism were, and how difficult was the position of those who wanted change: 'It is a very difficult country to move, Mr Hyndman, a very difficult country indeed, and one in which there is more disappointment to be looked for than success.'

The years of Chartism concluded an era which had witnessed the emergence of a class consciousness integrally related to the development of specifically working-class cultures. It was a class consciousness which expressed itself in different ways; with some important minority groups it was associated with a sophisticated radical critique of capitalist society,[3] but with all it was the recognition of the gulf between themselves, the labouring population, and those above them in the social scale. At its most elementary it was the 'them' and 'us' attitude which could also express itself in an inverted way in deference as well as in radical criticism and opposition. What was strongly marked by the middle of the century was the presence of working-class communities, often with distinctive regional and cultural characteristics.

After 1850, with the disintegration of an independent political movement there occurred the expansion of existing working-class organizations and institutions, as well as the establishment of new forms of self-help and encouragement of social activity. It was a process of 'warrening', as Edward Thompson has described it, creating self-help and defensive bodies to offset the continuous insecurities of everyday life in a capitalist society.[4] Such bodies as trade unions and friendly societies were already well established before 1850, as was the chapel, the temperance organization and benefit clubs; the second half of the century not only saw the expansion of these older forms of the warrening process but there was also the great expansion of the retail co-operative shop in the industrial North and more slowly in other parts of the country. Wholesale co-operation followed, and it became a major component of the Labour movement that was taking shape, although many co-operative societies were chary of becoming involved in radical politics. But in terms of offering educational and managerial opportunities, the co-operative movement was of major significance in working-class life in many areas of Britain, and it later added the establishment of the Women's Co-operative Guild in the 1880s: an important landmark in the history of the women's movement.

As material conditions slowly improved in the second half of the century, and it was a very uneven process between different groups among the manual workers, so there took place a steady thickening of this whole network of associations and institutions, with leisure activities beginning to occupy an increasing place in working men's lives. The working men's club movement, brass bands and whippet racing in the North, gardening clubs, and above all the phenomenon of mass sport watching from the 1880s, all contributed to the density of a working-class culture that was not impervious to outside ideas and influences, but which adapted middle-class values to their own, working-class, configuration. An intelligent working man of the better-off kind in the 1870s could be a trade unionist, a co-operator, a lay official of his chapel, and a member of a friendly society, a temperance body or a local working men's club. The pattern of membership would be largely determined by the region or urban area in which the individual lived. In South Wales the chapel would still have the strongest pull for many, as Sunday school teacher, lay preacher and later in life as chapel elder. In the coalfields of the North-east the union would have a more powerful influence, with the chapel still very important; in Lancashire the cotton unions and the co-operative movement would be central to many lives. In London, where both chapel and the co-operative movement were weaker than in the industrial North, the trade union would be important for the skilled worker as well as the friendly society, but the radical working men's club, or a debating forum or a secularist group might well be the strongest political attraction.

Whatever the regional differences, by the 1870s an ideology was developing that was common to most working men who were activist in some way or other, with the trade union normally the common denominator. It encompassed social and political attitudes whose horizons were firmly set within the boundaries of existing society; and as political democracy slowly extended after the 1867 Reform Act, and especially with the growing possibilities of election to local government bodies in the last quarter of the century, this labourist ideology struck deep roots in working-class consciousness. Labourism was a theory and practice which recognized the possibilities of social change within existing society, and which had no vision beyond existing society. It fully accepted the tradition, which went back beyond the Chartist movement, of the parliamentary variety of democracy as the practicable means of achieving its aims and objectives. By this time, of course, the meaning of the term 'democracy' had itself much weakened, and parliamentary democracy meant what bourgeois liberals understood it to mean. Labourism was the theory and practice of class collaboration; an attitude which in theory (always) and in practice (mostly) emphasized the fundamental unity of capital and labour. In political matters this meant an adherence to the Liberal Party and especially to the person of W. E. Gladstone, the 'People's William', but in industrial questions the issues were more complex. The foundations of this labourist philosophy lay in the work situation, the centre of proletarian life; and the phrase which summed up the labourist attitude was the slogan: 'A fair day's work for a fair day's pay'. Its meaning for trade unionists, however, was more complex than has sometimes been recognized. There was, on the one hand, an appreciation that fair dealing was available, or thought to be available, in capitalist society; but on the other, there was a stubborn insistence upon bargaining rights at the point of production. In the liberal–labour tradition, from the side of the working men, there was always an emphasis upon certain limited purposes and functions of trade unions. In no other area of life in capitalist society was 'independence' so clearly manifested; and while the ideological framework of labourism narrowed significantly the terms of reference within which industrial bargaining took place, there were some matters which came to be regarded as crucial for the preservation of trade unionism. Any threat, for example, to the legal status of unions always called forth great reserves of militant intransigence and class opposition. Any encroachment upon what were considered the traditional rights of organized workers evoked sharp responses. The insistence upon status and rights was the product of decades of conflict in the productive process with the employers of labour, who in most periods of modern British history have been much tougher and less accommodating than their political representatives and leaders. Trade unionism in the nineteenth century, after as well as before the Act of 1875, was always confronted with a steady and unrelenting hostility, not only from the employers of labour but from the propertied classes in general; and it is this which more than anything else shaped and moulded working-class attitudes and opinions. Whatever trade union leaders said in public about the need for the joint partnership of capital and labour the realities of life in the factory, workshop and mine meant a commitment to opposition, which many times involved industrial action, that contrasted sharply with the public pronouncements so often quoted to illustrate the caution and moderation of Victorian trade unionists.

These were contradictions which go far to explain the 'fractured' consciousness of the organized workers in nineteenth-century Britain. On the one hand, there was an 'economist' class consciousness continuously renewed from within the industrial sector; on the other, a pervasive sense and practice of collaboration in political affairs. The contrasts were striking, and they can be observed in every industrial sector of the nineteenth century economy, but it is the miners who exhibited more clearly than any other occupational group the labourist comprehension of their contemporary world.

The industrial history of the mining communities in the nineteenth century has been more adequately documented than for any other industrial group. Miners in most regions lived in villages, away from the mainstream of urban working-class life, and they developed a distinctive work, family and community culture. Conflict and bitter strife were endemic within the industrial relations of the industry, and it was not until the 1870s, and in most areas the 1880s, that stable trade unionism began to exist on a county basis. From then on most mining regions developed a massive sense of class solidarity that found expression in increasingly powerful union organizations. An industrial leadership had emerged by the last two decades of the nineteenth century that was notable both for its firmness on industrial issues and for its political moderation. The majority of miners' leaders were strongly attached to the Liberal Party, and parliamentary attitudes and practices had no more vigorous advocates than among the men of the mining communities.

How these things came about is not difficult to explain. On the industrial side the exploitation of the labour force was assisted by the monopoly control of the mine-owners in what were nearly always single-industry regions, and it was a control not only of jobs but also, in many areas, of housing; the geographical isolation of the miners from other groups of working people further contributed to the emergence of a highly developed sense of solidarity. Not that solidarity developed in any automatic or linear way. For many decades the miners found it impossible to establish viable unions. Their bargaining power, against the background of a continuous inwards migration to the coalfields, remained weak; and the constant pressures against militants by the mine-owners in terms both of jobs and houses were major obstacles to the establishment of permanent union organizations. Victimization, defeat after defeat in strikes, the repeated failure of local and regional unions – these were the common experiences of the mining communities before more or less stable unions entrenched themselves in the closing decades of the century. And once established there was no diminution in the bitterness with which industrial disputes were conducted.

The contrast between the miners' industrial class consciousness and their political attitudes was therefore sharply defined. In the year 1900, which saw the formation of the Labour Representation Committee (it became the Labour Party in 1906), there was no group of workers more completely committed to the Liberal Party than the miners. For one thing, the miners had always looked to Parliament for the redress of their many grievances. It was their firm conviction that only through the countervailing power of legislative action could they hope to offset the industrial strength enjoyed by the mine-owners; and parliamentarianism became stubbornly embedded in their political consciousness. Further, the gradual extension of political democracy at the local and regional level also encouraged the miners in their support for electoral politics. They mostly lived in rural areas, so had been excluded from the 1867 Reform Act, but they were enfranchized twenty years later, at a time when the franchise was also being extended to local bodies. Since the miners lived in single-occupation villages or towns they were able to concentrate their vote and take advantage of the new opportunities that were becoming available. The creation of school-boards in 1870; of county councils in 1888; of parish councils in 1893 and the abolition of the property qualification for boards of guardians in 1895; all were taken advantage of in the mining areas, so that the typical biography of a miners' leader between 1880 and the First World War would show election to most or all of the bodies mentioned above, and in some cases would also include election to Westminster. Out of eleven working-class MPs in 1885, all of them accepting the Liberal whip, six were miners.

There were other factors which encouraged political moderation. One undoubtedly was the roughness and toughness of the mine-owners, or their representatives, who, with some exceptions, were among the employers with the hardest faces and the most resolute of wills. To offset the monopoly power, as well as the callousness, of their masters, the miners needed political allies. Religion was another influence working in the same direction. There were large areas of working-class Britain that remained more or less untouched by religious beliefs and practices; the 'unconscious secularists' noted by the 1851 census. Among the working-class communities, however, in which religion, and especially the religion of Nonconformity, played an important part, the mining communities were especially notable. In England and Wales most mining areas were strongly influenced by the Nonconformist sects; and in some regions – Northumberland, Durham, Derbyshire and South Wales – the miner's lodge and the local chapel were almost interchangeable in terms of their social composition and their leadership. This was particularly true of the Primitive Methodist connection in England and the Baptists in Wales. The relationships between working-class religion and occupational groups were always complex and provide no easy generalizations; but on the whole the influence of the chapel tended towards political moderation and against violence in industrial disputes. The chapel also tended to encourage – outside the basic communal loyalty of the pit – certain individualist values on issues such as temperance, which after the 1860s tended to strengthen the links between the Liberal Party and the mining communities.[5]

It is important to appreciate how tough and tenacious the labourist tradition was among the mining areas. It was a vigorous, reforming tradition with nothing soft or sentimental about it in the matter of the interests of the miners. The leaders through whom labourist attitudes were expressed had been the pioneers of trade unionism in their younger days. They had often suffered victimization and ejection from company houses but in the end it was they who built the unions as stable organizations. They were tough and hard negotiators on industrial issues; their record in mine rescue work was usually outstanding; and their service to their fellow men was for all to see, not only in union affairs, but when the opportunities developed, on the school-board, local council or board of guardians. And by the end of the century these veterans of the struggle could look back and underline the material progress that had been made in the condition of the miners and their families. The intellectual and political horizons of these miners' leaders were sharply limited and in the closing decades of the century they were always ready to pay fulsome tributes to the 'People's William'; and once the relations between the Liberal Party and the politically aware of working men, including the miners, had come to be firmly established, momentum carried the political attitudes involved well into the twentieth century. When socialist ideas began to come back into British politics in the 1880s, after an absence of some thirty years, the alliance between the Liberal Party and most active trade unionists had already become an effective working arrangement; and in spite of the Liberal Party's reluctance to meet the growing demands in the 1890s for more working-class candidates, it was not an alliance that was easily undermined.

There were certain characteristics of this labourist tradition that require emphasis for they have remained embedded within ideas and attitudes to the present day. One was that the labourist ideology was most clearly defined among the more skilled strata of the working population although skill was not always the determining factor; the degree of control over work-processes was also important. What is interesting and significant is that when hitherto unorganized workers – often those whose labour was casual – obtained some measure of organization they demonstrated the same kinds of concern, and the same attitudes, as their skilled brothers had long been exhibiting. There were fewer of them in relation to their total numbers than the better-off workers; but almost all who were gradually brought within the active body politic before 1914 demonstrated the pervasiveness of a broad labourist approach to political and social questions. This labourist tradition, it must be further emphasized, was predominantly male-dominated, and in its social attitudes it was profoundly conservative. The radical ideas on religion, the family, the relationships between the sexes and those between parents and children, which had been part of the Owenite movement before the mid 1840s, almost completely disappeared during the third quarter of the century.

These middle decades of the 1840s and 1850s represent a turning point not only in working-class politics but in working-class ideology in the broadest sense of its interpretation. The vigorous anti-capitalist critique which the socialists of the 1820s had developed and which was to be found in popular expression in widely read journals, such as the *Poor Man's Guardian*, *The Crisis* and the *Pioneer*, largely petered out by the end of the 1830s, leaving a widespread but more vague anti-capitalist ethos which still permeated much of the Chartist movement; but this also had died away, except in an increasingly labourist sense, after Ernest Jones' failure to revive Chartism in the early 1850s. There was a parallel collapse of radical social attitudes during the 1840s, and where they continued they assumed mostly sectarian forms. Bradlaugh's secularism was allied to a vigorous political radicalism, but except for the birth-control episode of the late 1870s, it tended to be a traditional movement of protest, although certainly the most principled of the middle decades.

Just as there was little in the labourist tradition for the 30–40 per cent of the working population who lived on or below the margin of poverty, or for women specifically, so the leisure activities that gradually emerged during the second half of the century were male-dominated – in most cases exclusively male – and within the male working class they were available, in the majority of instances, to the better-off rather than to the poor or the very poor: for whom the beer-house and their wives' bodies were the main consolations of life. The cumulative effects of industrialization pushed women either into the very restricting round of married life, child-bearing and child-rearing, or, given the large surplus of women under the age of fifty, into the lowest paid employment or into dependent positions within the family group. The majority of men in the skilled and semi-skilled groups, by the end of the century, had a considerable range of social, political, educational or leisure activities available to them while women were mostly confined to the networks of their family life or to religion. When libraries began to be collected around the mining lodges of South Wales, they were not open to women; and in general, over the country as a whole, the typical auto-didact of the nineteenth century was a man. Industrialization brought cultural impoverishment to all groups within the working class in the nineteenth century, but cultural deprivation was more pronounced among women than men.

[20]

The ideology of labourism encouraged working people to maintain their sense of class, another way of describing their independence and self-respect; but it also involved the acceptance of a subordinate role in political society. A still much debated question among social historians concerns the degree to which middle-class ideas and values permeated or dominated working-class attitudes in the mid and late Victorian decades. It is not historically reasonable to argue for a direct or unmediated indoctrination of middle-class values, since all ideas and social attitudes derive in the first place from the given work situation and the life style; and whatever influences there are coming from outside the class they will be refracted through the general experience of the working-class community. In working-class politics, however, there is little doubt about the growing importance of what Bottomore has called the 'weaker version' of the dominant ideology thesis: the capacity of a dominant ideology, in the present context that of the Victorian middle classes, 'to inhibit and confuse the development of a counter-ideology of a subordinate class'.[6] Inhibition and confusion was compounded by the general mediocrity of English intellectual life in the second half of the nineteenth century, particularly that which concerned social questions. The great majority of intellectuals remained uncritical, conformist and complacent. When neo-Hegelianism became fashionable during the third quarter of the century, its most radical version was the liberalism of T. H. Green, who emphasized the moral purposes of the state, the importance of education and the evil of drink. John Stuart Mill was moving towards a liberal collectivism in the closing years of his life and he espoused a number of radical causes, above all feminism; but his influence, except for his impact upon Sidney Webb, and some of Webb's Fabian colleagues, declined quite sharply in the last quarter of the century. The Positivists, Harrison and Beesley, whose defence of the Paris Commune was in an authentic radical tradition, then fell away from working-class politics and became involved in literary and Positivist concerns. They were probably the lost intellectuals of a genuinely radical movement; for although Ruskin was to have much more influence upon working men than anyone else of his time, his ardent critique of industrial society remained partial and his positive suggestions for change ludicrous. Only William Morris, who acknowledged Ruskin as his master 'before the days of my practical socialism' moved beyond the categories of romantic protest to accept 'that amidst all this filth of civilisation the seeds of great change, what we others call Social-Revolution, were beginning to germinate'. Morris, in the same passage, further commented that his recognition of the practical possibilities of a new social order saved him from 'crystallising into a mere railer against "progress"' on the one hand, and from middle-class utopianism on the other. But such was the intellectual weakness of the radical left that after Morris's death in 1896 his acceptance of a revolutionary socialist position was quickly overlaid with misinterpretations and misunderstandings. The revolutionary content of his writings was ignored, and certainly not developed; the responsibility can only be that of his fellow socialists in the generations who came after.[7]

3

The early decades: 1900–26

By the end of the nineteenth century Britain was an old industrial country. It had been a long time in the making, and the processes of economic change were very unevenly divided between industries, and within industries. As late as the 1851 census most of those who worked with their hands were outside the factory proper, the main concentration of which was in the textile areas of Lancashire. The census recorded more shoemakers than coalminers, more tailors than ironworkers, with agriculture still the largest occupation in total numbers, followed by domestic service. The next fifty years saw a rapid expansion in the main staple industries: textiles, coal, iron and steel, heavy engineering and shipbuilding; and by 1900 trade union organization was largely concentrated in these export-orientated industries. Before the upsurge of New Unionism in the late 1880s, the percentage of male workers organized was only about 10 per cent, but by the end of the next decade the proportion of organized adult male workers (excluding domestic servants and farmers) had increased to around 25 per cent; and in 1910 it had further increased to some 30 per cent. Unionization was heavily concentrated among the workers in cotton and coal, some 40 per cent of the total in the first decade of the twentieth century, with other concentrations among skilled workers in the metal working trades and shipbuilding.

It was these long-established unions, many with considerable craft control over their working conditions, and set firmly in their local communities, that constituted the heartland of the Labour movement as it was to develop during the twentieth century; and it was these unions and these communities that were often to prove impervious to the new ideas of socialism that were beginning to circulate in the last two decades of the nineteenth century. Trade union members had usually acquired some degree of political radicalism, and it was precisely their defined adherence to the liberal–labour position that steadily resisted the impact of socialist ideas and propaganda. It was, indeed, often easier to make converts to socialism from the more free-wheeling radical and secularist groups in London and the big cities, or from those without previous political commitment, than among the workers in the well-established trades and the traditional working-class communities; a phenomenon to be observed in other countries, and in other times.

It is an interesting question to explain why socialist ideas began to be discussed again in the 1880s after their more or less complete absence since the early 1850s. If ideas were a simple reflection of objective circumstances the socialist revival could certainly have occurred earlier; for the poverty of many groups and the widespread insecurity of employment and living standards had always been present. There had been stirrings and rumblings a decade earlier, but it was the coming together of Henry George, coercion in Ireland, imperialist adventures in the Middle East and a few lively personalities that produced the first small implantation. Poverty as a social phenomenon began to be rediscovered; the extraordinary public reaction to *The Bitter Cry of Outcast London* was remarkable in its unexpectedness, and as A. J. Balfour, a perceptive witness, commented at the Industrial Remuneration Conference in 1885, it was the social condition of society and not its political constitution and structure that was the increasing concern of contemporary commentators. Tom Mann became a socialist through reading Henry

George and John Ruskin, and it was George who destroyed belief in the 'iron laws' of political economy that provided a yoke for so many in these years. As the moderate Christian Socialist, Stewart Headlam, explained in 1882: until he read George's attack on Malthus 'he had found it very difficult to see how any reforms could do away with poverty. The author, however, had pointed out that Malthus had no grounds for his belief'. What George showed was that poverty was the result of man-made laws, and that what man had put together could equally be undone, and replaced. It was not necessary to be limited to George's own specific remedies, which is why so many moved beyond George to socialism.[1]

Socialism was part of this new attack upon orthodox political economy. *Why are the Many Poor?* was the title of the first Fabian Society pamphlet in 1884, and by the end of the decade Charles Booth had begun to document in massive detail the economic and social causes of destitution. The main thrust of socialist progaganda in the 1880s – and we are referring here to a few hundred individuals – came from the Social Democratic Federation and to a lesser extent from the Socialist League (until the anarchists took over); and it was these two bodies which attracted those ardent spirits whose names quickly became well known. It was in the next decade that socialism took on a more popular colouring and reached out to still small but significant numbers of working people. These were years when socialism became a way of life for the dedicated who argued and debated not only how to make socialists but how socialists themselves should live. For those who caught the vision of a new society without poverty and exploitation it was an exhilarating time to be living.

There were large theoretical differences between the various socialist groups: the Marxist Social Democratic Federation (SDF), the gradualist Fabian Society which discouraged a working-class adherence as well as membership outside London, and the earnest proselytizing Independent Labour Party (ILP) whose foundation conference was at Bradford in 1893. The SDF vigorously debated the implications of short-term reforms – palliatives they were called – and they continued to worry about the corrupting influences of social reforms upon the social consciousness of their fellow workers. The problem was how the workers were to be moved away from their traditional 'common sense' towards a recognition that only the abolition of the whole capitalist order would bring true dignity and real personal worth: a question that has remained with the Marxist left to our own days. For the ILP there were no serious problems of this kind. The social evils that disfigured and disgraced Britain must be ended, and solutions could only be piecemeal in general, and often at first obtained only at the local level. It was the Fabian Society, accepting dogmatically the 'inevitability of gradualness' − although the actual phrase was not yet used − who produced many of the criticisms of existing institutions and social policies, and offered reformist blueprints for the future. As Engels remarked in 1893 in the course of a critique of the Fabian Society: 'with great industry they have produced amid all sorts of rubbish some good propagandist writings as well, and in fact the best kind the English have produced'.

In their day-to-day affairs, in practical matters and on practical problems, the differences in the ways in which social problems were approached were much less marked among the various socialist groups than their theoretical disagreements. The minimum wage, the eight-hour day, the feeding of school children and their medical inspection, better equipment for the board schools, old age pensions and more liberal attitudes on the part of Poor Law guardians, these became the planks of local political campaigns. The tangible benefits of 'municipal socialism', which included the Fair Wage clause for local government contract work, were becoming increasingly obvious. And where, in the same town or region, the ILP existed alongside the SDF, political sense pushed them together in joint campaigns. By the end of the century there was a socialist presence in many parts of British society; a good deal more vocal than its actual numbers might have suggested and as yet with only a minor implantation among the trade unions. The organized labour movement remained for the most part labourist within the liberal tradition.[2]

It was, no doubt, inevitable in a country with the historical political traditions of Britain and with a social composition overwhelmingly proletarian that an independent working-class party would at some point emerge. The question was one of timing, and there is no reason to believe that it had to happen in 1900. If the judiciary had been less prejudiced, and the Liberal Party more intelligent during the previous decade, the beginnings of the break with traditional Liberalism might have been further delayed. When, however, the present Labour Party effectively established itself in 1900, the central and dominating components of the new organization were the trade unions, all of whom wanted increased working-class representation in Parliament but almost none of whom were socialists. The Labour Representation Committee of 1900, which became the Labour Party in 1906, was manoeuvred into existence by the socialist leadership of the ILP who were prepared, at the time and subsequently, to accept large-scale compromises on political issues in order to develop an independent Labour presence, both in the country and at Westminster. The federal structure of the new party meant that while the activist leadership was mostly socialist, of the ILP persuasion since the Marxists soon withdrew, the voting majority always came from the trade unions. And so it has remained. In this crucial matter the British Labour movement differed notably from most of those on the European continent where the political parties of the left either directly controlled or largely influenced the trade unions. In Britain, the compact entered into by the unions with the small socialist groupings emerged from decades of labourist theory and practice that was to endure, with modifications, throughout the twentieth century. What gradually emerged was a Labour socialism: a socialist rhetoric fused with the labourist values of the Liberal era before 1914. The term 'socialist rhetoric' must not be thought of as pejorative. The early pioneers of Labour socialism – Keir Hardie, Ramsay MacDonald, Philip Snowden, Fred Jowett – no less than their rank and file were passionately committed to the attack upon the harshness and the constant insecurity of the grim environment in which so many working people

[27]

lived and died. The Labour socialists offered a vision of a decent, humane society, and they encouraged, and received, a commitment of great personal sacrifice from the many who responded. It was the achievement of office that later was to corrupt, the result, among many other reasons, of an incapacity to appreciate the nature of power in a capitalist society.

The founding conference of the Labour Representation Committee was in 1900 and its history in the next few years was primarily concerned with electoral tactics; the attempt by the SDF to fasten a socialist commitment upon the new organization failed. The SDF withdrew, leaving the ILP as the only important socialist group providing political leadership. The secret agreement of 1903 with the Liberal Party on parliamentary constituencies which was negotiated by Ramsey MacDonald and agreed to by Keir Hardie was a recognition of the electoral difficulties of breaking into the two-party system, and a further indication of the political compromises the socialist leadership of the ILP were prepared to make. When the Labour Representation Committee won twenty-nine seats in the general election of 1906 the Labour Party had arrived; and between the opening of the new Parliament and the outbreak of war in August 1914 much of the energies of leading figures such as Ramsay MacDonald were absorbed within the walls of Westminster.

This first period of Labour socialism saw firmly established the main characteristics of the Parliamentary Labour Party and, to a more diffuse extent, of the Labour Party in the country at large. The primacy of Parliament in political strategy was unquestioned; a legacy of the years of labourism that has been steadily added to in the twentieth century. Already before 1900 the gains that had been made at local level had confirmed the new possibilities of social change, and in the early years of the new century it was Parliament, after the Liberal victory of 1906, which overturned the anti-union Taff Vale judgement, and which introduced improved legislation for the children of the poor and the old age pension for those of seventy and over. These advances confirmed the general belief among reformers of all kinds that the government in a political democracy were in full control of the state and state power, and that upon the Government's ability to legislate there were no effective limitations. The theory was based upon the postulate of the neutrality of the state: that any administration which took power was *ipso facto* in full and complete control of its legislative programme, the implementation of which, given a majority in the House of Commons, would not be seriously hindered. A passage from an early Fabian pamphlet by Bernard Shaw, *The Impossibilities of Anarchism* (1893), makes explicit the Fabian theory of the state, and its concomitant, the inevitability of social progress in a political democracy:

It is easy to say, Abolish the State; but the State will sell you up, lock you up, blow you up, knock you down, bludgeon, shoot, stab, hang – in short abolish you, if you lift a hand against it. Fortunately, there is, as we have seen a fine impartiality about the policeman and the soldier, who are the cutting edge of the State power. They take their wages and obey their orders without asking questions. If those orders are to demolish the homestead of every peasant who refuses to take bread out of his children's mouths in order that his landlord may have the money to spend as an idle gentleman in London, that soldier obeys. But if his orders were to help the police to pitch his Lordship into Holloway Gaol until he has paid an Income Tax of twenty shillings on every pound of his unearned income, the soldier would do that with equal devotion to duty, and perhaps with a certain private zest that might be lacking in the other case. Now these orders come ultimately from the State – meaning, in this country, the House of Commons. A House of Commons consisting of 660 gentlemen and 10 workmen will order the soldier to take money from the people for the landlords. A House of Commons consisting of 660 workmen and 10 gentlemen will probably, unless the 660 are fools, order the soldier to take the money from the landlords for the people. With this hint I leave the matter, in the full conviction that the State, in spite of the Anarchists, will continue to be used against the people by the classes until it is used by the people against the classes with equal ability and equal resolution.

The conviction that the state is neutral as between the different political parties who gain a parliamentary majority at Westminster has remained central to the thinking of the Labour Party throughout the twentieth century. It has been accepted broadly by the left within the Party as well as the right. And when things go wrong with the decisions and policies of progressive governments, as they invariably do, the explanation is usually some simple conspiracy theory of an international bankers' ramp, or the hostility and misinformation techniques of the media; not irrelevant considerations but certainly not the whole story; and all expounded with a great deal of sound and fury. For what has never been properly taken into account by the Labour Party and its supporters in the country is the nature and character of economic power in Britain, and the relationship between power and the ruthless class consciousness of those who are the great owners of property. The Labour leadership have always assumed that the Parliamentary game will be played according to its rules by all those involved. There are, it must be admitted, good reasons for these beliefs, since the Labour leaders have done little if anything to cause the propertied classes of Britain to abandon their qualified acceptance of the rules; and the further back in time the more likely it is to find both political and industrial leaders of the Labour movement who have approached the British constitution and those responsible for its workings with respect bordering upon deference. Alexander Macdonald, a miners' leader who died in 1881, was described as simmering with satisfaction at 'holding easy converse with a live lord', and he was only one of the first upon whom the magic of status worked with powerful effect. The labourist tradition in its industrial relations tended always towards conciliation and arbitration, and not confrontation, but the hostility of employers in most industries to unions in general meant that negotiations had to be firm and shrewd. There were no such restraints upon the political side of the movement; and what became known as the 'aristocratic embrace' was only a crude approximation for a much more subtle and encompassing influence by the well established upon the new arrivals in positions of political power. It was a debilitating and corrupting process that was not limited to Westminster but extended right through the political system down to municipal levels. The history of Labour in local government in the twentieth century is a mixed story of integrity and reformist achievement of no mean order alongside financial corruption and administrative feebleness.

Between the general election of 1906 and the outbreak of war in 1914 the Parliamentary Labour Party took shape. The Party was involved first in certain items of legislation which were crucial to its purposes, and above all, the necessary measures to remedy the Taff Vale decision against the unions. After 1910 the PLP was largely concerned with the power-struggles between the Tories and the Liberal Government, and by this time the acceptance of all the conventions at Westminster had steadily emasculated its parliamentary performance, and its growing flabbiness was in sharp contrast with the developing mass unrest in the country as a whole. The increasing personal attacks upon Ramsay MacDonald were part of a more general scepticism about Parliament and its usefulness. G. K. Chesterton, in the newly established *Daily Herald*, summed up a widespread attitude:

> It would not have made the slightest difference for good or ill, to the future of anything or anybody, if the tiger had eaten him. There would have been a Liberal member for Leicester instead, who would have made the same speeches, given exactly the same votes; and, if he were the usual successful soapboiler, would have eclipsed MacDonald in everything except good looks.[3]

The decade before the beginning of war was an extraordinarily lively period of socialist thinking, and mass discontent; in sharp contrast with the feebleness of the Parliamentary Labour Party. The Boer War had stimulated the discussion of imperialism, and this was continued with a vigorous opposition to British policy in Egypt. E. D. Morel's exposé of Belgian atrocities in the Congo, a growing opposition to the international arms market, an increasing interest in India, all contributed to a new awareness of the international ramifications of the world capitalist system. These ideas were given their most complete expression in H. N. Brailsford's *The War of Steel and Gold* which appeared in 1914; it was a volume which educated a whole generation of young socialists during the war years, and guided their search for a postwar policy.

This upsurge of socialist ideas mixed with the growth of critical thinking about Victorian Britain – roughly from the mid 1890s – also found expression in new approaches towards the political education of working people. What we have in these years is both the attempt to channel working-class education into the safe and liberal outlets of the Workers Educational Association and Ruskin College, and the development of working-class initiatives from below; and it is the latter only which made its contribution to the socialist movement – and a considerable contribution it was. Within the well-established Social Democratic Federation there appeared a new generation of Marxists of whom Theodore Rothstein was outstanding. He had arrived in England in 1891 and became active in socialist politics from the middle of the decade. In 1895 he married Anna Kahan, sister of Zelda, who was herself to become a well-known militant in the SDF. Rothstein brought a European sophistication into the movement and he was especially important in sustaining the anti-imperialist and anti-war groups within the SDF, against the jingoism of Hyndman and the widespread social patriotism within the general Labour movement; and down to 1914 Rothstein remained one of the left's most versatile, erudite and persuasive writers and propagandists. But this whole period, from the late 1890s to the beginning of war, witnessed new forms of class activity and political education. In 1903 the Socialist Labour Party was founded as a breakaway from the SDF. It was orthodox Marxist in inspiration, as interpreted by the American Daniel De Leon. The SLP accepted short-term reforms, but its main emphasis was upon the socialist education of working people, by the raising of their class consciousness. To this end the SLP pioneered new ways of self-education. Their aim was to create worker-intellectuals who could engage in socialist agitation on the factory floor and at street corner meetings. The SLP rejected the parliamentarianism of the 'labour fakirs'; they insisted upon a high level of discipline based upon what later became known as democratic centralism; and in the years before 1914 they exerted an influence out of proportion to their numbers. They were mostly centred in and around Glasgow, but they had outlying posts in other towns. We have, in the memoirs of Tom Bell, a remarkable account of the new methods of workers' education. Bell himself conducted classes for fifteen winters in Glasgow, from 1905 to 1920, with only one year's break in London and Liverpool:

> Our method in the classes was to open with an inaugural survey of the whole field we proposed to traverse, and to make the workers familiar with the subject as a whole; the textbooks etc. which included *Wage Labour and Capital; Value, Price and Profit; Capital;* and H. de B. Gibbins' *Industry in England* and Buckle's *History of Civilisation.* Each student was given a series of definitions of terms used by Marx. These had to be studied, memorised and discussed thoroughly, for perhaps the first four weeks. The student would study *Wage Labour and Capital* at home. At the class we would read it over paragraph by paragraph, round the class. This practice aimed at helping the students to speak fluently and grammatically. At the following class meeting questions would be put and answered, and the points raised thoroughly understood by everyone, the results of each lesson being summarised by the leader. This method was applied in the same way to industrial history. Later on, simple lessons on historical materialism and formal logic were added. So that, after six months of this, every worker who went through the entire session came out a potential tutor for other classes.[4]

It was a tough, hard political school conducted with the fervour and dedication of the Scottish Calvinist tradition. The turnover of party members was high, and the political sectarianism of party life, which included the heresy hunting that has remained an integral part of the hard left throughout the twentieth century, could easily have fallen into the pit of political vacuity that was the fate of the Socialist Party of Great Britain, another breakaway from the Social Democratic Federation. What saved the SLP from historical irrelevance, and gave it the necessary dynamic to move beyond its own little sect and make contact with ordinary manual workers, was their acceptance of De Leon's insistence upon industrial unionism.

In 1907 the inaugural conference of the Advocates of Industrial Unionism was held in Birmingham, the result of several years' debate and discussion; and the SLP, which refused to allow its members to hold any kind of office in the trade union movement, increased its propaganda on the factory floor and at factory gate meetings. Members were recruited in the Argyle Motor Works, Alexandria, and the Albion Motor Works, Scotstown, both to be centres of the shop stewards' movement on Clydeside during the war years, but their greatest success was in the Singer Sewing Machine works which employed over 10,000 workers. Most of these were semi-skilled or unskilled, and not unionized, and by the spring of 1911 the SLP in its union role had recruited some 4,000 workers. In March 1911 a female union member was dismissed, and the three-week strike which followed included thirty-seven of the firm's forty-one departments. The skilled toolmakers, organized by the Amalgamated Society of Engineers, remained at work. The failure of the strike after three weeks led to the successive dismissal of all the leading shop stewards, most of whom were SLP members, and they now became scattered throughout Glasgow and its region's industrial factories: a crucial prelude to the industrial history of Clydeside from 1915 on.

The main strength of the SLP remained in the Glasgow area, but it had a few branches elsewhere: in London, Tyneside and half a dozen other towns. These included Oxford where a new movement for class-based workers' education originated following the Ruskin College strike of 1909. Ruskin College had been established in 1899 by two

Americans, and by 1906 the College, which was largely independent of the University, had a considerable part of its student body financially supported by various labour organizations, mostly trade unions. The College, not surprisingly given the changing climate of opinion within the Labour movement, began to take on a socialist colouring. The governing body was a mix of university representatives and trade union officials, with Denis Hird, a socialist of the Social Democratic Federation persuasion, as principal. Most of the academic staff were liberal, and shared the general university belief that education should be 'non-partisan', the Oxford approach which it was assumed conveyed to its own students 'a wide outlook' and a 'synoptic mind'. These were phrases used by a report on *Oxford and Working Class Education* published in December 1908 and which, together with Lord Curzon's *Principles and Methods of University Reform* of 1909, provided the basic texts for the discussion by their betters of the problems of educating the masses, or more accurately, the élite groups from among the working people. There should be, for instance, a sharing of the facilities of the existing universities including what Curzon called the 'indescribable glamour' of college life. The central problem, of course, was the content of what should be taught, and it was here that tensions began to develop within Ruskin College itself. In February 1909 there was published the first number of the *Plebs* magazine which among other aims attacked the idea of the absorption of the College by the University, and called for its control by the trade union movement. The developing critical situation inside Ruskin led to the imposed resignation of Denis Hird and the famous strike of Ruskin students at the end of March 1909; this in turn provided the basis for the establishment of the Central Labour College in the following August.[5]

The first number of *Plebs* had carried an article from Noah Ablett, a young miner from the Rhondda Valley. Ablett had been sent to Ruskin by the South Wales Miners Federation and had just completed his second year at Ruskin. In the years which followed, he exemplified the new spirit of the times as well as any of his contemporaries. He was indefatigable in establishing Marxist educational classes throughout the Welsh coalfield. He was elected to the executive committee of the Federation at the beginning of 1911, and later in that year played an important part in the discussions and negotiations over the Cambrian Combine strike. He became a member of the Unofficial Reform Committee which Noah Rees had originally initiated and which had W. H. Mainwaring as its secretary; and it was out of this group that there came the famous pamphlet *The Miners' Next Step*. Ablett and his colleagues were never simon-pure syndicalists, in the strict meaning of the term, but there was much convergence between their ideas and the syndicalist insistence on the primacy of industrial action and the self-reliance of the working people on their own revolutionary efforts.

We are confronted with a series of paradoxes in the decade or so before 1914. The Parliamentary Labour Party was becoming increasingly discredited, while at the local level the number of Labour and trade union representatives on local councils and other bodies such as boards of guardians was increasing steadily, although their distribution was notably patchy throughout the country. But it was this thickening of the Labour presence in the years before 1914 that was training local leaderships, which were to prove important when Labour made considerable local and regional electoral gains in the postwar world.[6] Nor must the achievements of 'municipal socialism' be underrated. For most manual workers, of course, who were in any way organized or socially active, it was the traditional institutions of labourism – the co-operative society, the chapel, the trade union branch or lodge, the friendly society – together with the growing opportunities for some kind of leisure activity which continued to occupy their time outside working hours. But there was also at this period a massive wave of industrial unrest of a quite unprecedented kind. The disillusionment with moderate trade unionism – most union leaders were still of the labourist kind – and with moderate parliamentarianism was compounded by rising prices, a pressure on real wages, and relatively full employment; but these were not new phenomena in industrial history, singly or in combination. Without the political dimension, at this time the propagandist activities of the industrial unionists and syndicalists, it is unlikely that the upsurge in strike activity would have been quite so powerful. From 1900 to 1907 the number of working days lost reached only 4 million in one year, and in most years were well below this figure. Then, in 1908, the figures jumped to over 10.75 million, fell back in 1909 to just under 3 million, rose to around 10 million in both 1910 and 1911 and reached nearly 41 million in 1912, with nearly 12 million in 1913. At the beginning of the strike movement it looked as though it was the continuation of the New Unionism of the late 1880s, in that workers on the waterfront played a significant part in the early stages. But this was not to continue, and the greater part of those involved in these turbulent years were rail-waymen, engineering workers, semi-skilled and unskilled outside the traditional craft unions, workers in certain of the new factory-type industries such as chemicals, rubber and paints, and two groups of strongly organized workers, the miners and cotton-weavers. In August 1911 the four railway unions called a national strike – largely to control an increasingly restive rank and file – and although the stoppage was not complete, the Government reacted swiftly with a new settlement. In the next year the Miners Federation began the biggest national strike ever seen in Britain, which again was met by some measures of concession. The institutional results of this massive strike action were a considerable increase in total union membership – from 2.5 million in 1910 to just over 4 million in 1914 – and the lessening of the importance in the trade union movement as a whole of coal and cotton because of the growth of the transport and general labour groups. The most successful of the general unions – the Workers Union – had no more than 5,000 members in 1910 and nearly 160,000 by the closing months of 1914.

The complexities of the strike movement during these years have produced conflicting explanations. At one end of the spectrum there are those who adhere to a rather simple correlation with the movements of real wages, and at the other end those who relate militancy in the industrial sector with a more general crisis in society: the strange death of liberal England as it was once described. It was without question for those in middle and later ages of life a time when society appeared to be experiencing convulsions unknown in the Victorian years. The suffragette desecration of the putting greens of golf courses was no doubt regarded by many of the upper classes with as much horror as the tragic immolation of Emily Davidson on Derby day 1913; but suffragette violence was the work of quite a small group of mainly middle- and upper-class women, and it was not supported by a majority of women of all classes. The suffrage movement was, however, sustained by a significant, if minority section of the Labour movement; and there was a working-class women's component to the movement – in London and Lancashire, for example – that is often overlooked.

The Irish problem in Ulster was undoubtedly a more serious threat to the stability of state. The 'Curragh' incident[7] exposed brutally the willingness of sections of the propertied classes to fight to hold what they had, but there were still many compromises that were practicable between the various groups of the governing classes. In the short and middle term British imperialism would have found a way, and it was unlikely before the war began to have gone as far as the settlement of 1922. The industrial discontent, however, had some elements that were new. After the obliteration of Chartism the shaping and moulding of the working class had been remarkably successful, and for half a century after 1848 there was very little to worry their masters. What was new in the years immediately preceding 1914 was the size of the strike movement for which there was no comparable explosion in contemporary Europe, the violence which accompanied a number of the strike actions and the presence of uncompromising working-class agitators and propagandists expounding new doctrines which had nothing to do with the traditional labourism that had been part of the trade union movement for so long.

The nature and character of the violence of these years would repay further investigation. Violence in mining strikes in general and against blacklegs in particular was hardly a new phenomenon – nor was police brutality – but now in South Wales there were attacks on the homes of pit managers and on pit-head installations; and violence was not limited to the coalfields. The leadership of Tom Mann in the August 1911 strike in Liverpool, and the tumultuous state of Liverpool, provided new dimensions to working-class discontent. The spread of the gospel of industrial unionism – the reliance by the workers upon themselves – and the power in united action presented employers and the British state with what appeared to be quite new problems with higher levels of risk. When the Webbs returned from a world tour in 1912 they wrote of 'an awakened England' and certainly this is how it appeared to contemporaries. The formation of the Triple Alliance in April 1914 had been some years in the making and it was an illustration of the potentially dangerous movements that were entering industrial politics. The Alliance was an association of the National Transport Workers Federation, which had brought together in 1910 all the leading unions in transport except for the railways, the National Union of Railwaymen, which was the result of the merger in 1913 of three of the five principal unions on the railways, and the Miners Federation of Great Britain, which had won the eight-hour-day Act in 1908 and district minimum wages in 1912. The Alliance, it should be noted, had strictly limited aims in spite of the syndicalist views of a minority of its leaders. The highly alarmist comments in the press concealed the differences among the leadership as to aims and purposes, as well as the moderation of many of its leaders. In certain circumstances, of course, it might have developed a considerable degree of industrial power.[8]

There were some sectors of British industry that were passing through a period of considerable technical change, and it can be accepted that the changing labour process in certain industries contributed to the industrial problems, and the industrial militancy, of the workers involved. For example, in engineering – a general term which covered a wide selection of metal-using processes – the possibilities of mass production techniques were present from the 1890s, and the struggle for job control by the craft workers was a central part of the industrial history to 1914, and after. To what extent the industrial power of organized unionism restricted the investment strategies of employers is a much-debated question. Certainly a range of skilled crafts were able to maintain their control over the work process; the case of printing is common to a number of advanced economies in the two or three decades before 1914. In the United Kingdom employers' reactions to the price and profit falls of the last quarter of the nineteenth century was often not a capital-deepening investment but a more efficient use of existing equipment; and this undoubtedly encouraged the dependence upon skilled labour which helped to strengthen the position of the craft unions. It was never a simple historical change for the reason that the factors involved in any one industry were not necessarily common to others: market structures and average size of firms were not uniform; and the consequences of the interaction of business strategy and union or labour force response sometimes encouraged militancy, and sometimes not. Skilled metal workers tended to be radicalized by the technological changes of the late nineteenth century – which continued in an uneven way through the first half of the twentieth century and into the years after the Second World War – but industrial militancy is always the result of a complex of factors, of which the political dimension is usually important.[9] It is necessary further to recall that in spite of the new levels of industrial unrest in the years immediately before the outbreak of war, three quarters of the work-force still remained outside the trade unions; and there were both coercive and moderating factors playing upon those engaged in industrial struggle. The business community, and the various parts of the state apparatus, met this much increased activity on the part of the industrial workers by well-tried and traditional methods: the widespread use of blackleg labour and their protection by the security forces of the state; by constant and continuous misrepresentation in the press; and by unremitting pressure upon the moderate political and union leaders. The hunger experienced by strikers' families was always helpful. And at the same time there was a minority trend within the business world which looked to conciliation and arbitration as the solutions to industrial problems. There had been some institutional developments in the second half of the nineteenth century, and A. J. Mundella, president of the Board of Trade in Gladstone's last

Government, pushed things along. An expanded labour department became a centre for advanced liberal ideas, favourable to union organization and inevitably much criticized by the employers' side. Its expertise carried over into the twentieth century and the Board of Trade, after the Liberal victory of 1906, developed and expanded its conciliation procedures. In 1907 Lloyd George appointed Sir George Askwith with a roving commission within the areas of industrial disputes. We have here the further development of what Middlemass has characterized as the corporate bias within British society: the acceptance by employer's associations, trade unions and the state of the resolution of industrial and political crises by discussion, conciliation and arbitration. Middlemass dates these developments from the experiences of the First World War and in his words, 'institutional collaboration supplemented the party parliamentary system and produced a measure of harmony in the interwar years'; and he further argued that the basic political equilibrium produced continued through the Second World War and for two decades after. It is an attractive thesis representing half the truth but not the whole truth. It can be looked at from another perspective: that in the oldest industrial society the considerable strength of organized labour was held in check, first by the relations within industry, and in particular and most important by the moderate and compromising attitudes of the trade union leaders; and second, by the failure, until 1945, of the party of the working class, in a society with a working-class majority, to achieve effective command of parliament at Westminster. Corporate bias had undoubtedly diminished social tensions; it has also left the fundamentals of British society – the ownership of the means of production, the distribution of income and even more striking, the distribution of wealth – unchanged in any significant way.[10]

The weakness of the politics of Labour was strikingly illustrated at the outset of war in August 1914 when the great majority of working people, along with all other classes, were caught up in a great wave of jingoism that overwhelmed the industrial struggles – which had not been diminishing – and the small minority of socialists and pacifists who opposed the war on political and/or moral grounds. The early years of war in particular illustrated once again the ways in which contradictory ideas can jostle together in people's minds. Coal-miners joined up in large numbers from the beginning of the war, at the same time as industrial relations remained as bitter as ever for those who stayed in the pits, or for those who came back; and the number of days lost in strike action was considerable. Elsewhere in industry there was rising militancy from the beginning of 1915; on the Clyde and in certain other centres of heavy industry such as Sheffield. The craft unions mostly strengthened their control over their work processes; and the shop-steward movement, again especially in the metal industries, proved a vigorous training ground for militants. Almost all the Labour and trade union leaders supported the war; some with a marked jingoistic fervour, as did the majority of ordinary people. But the impact of these four years of horrific bloodshed was to be considerable, often in a curiously delayed way. By the second half of the twenties the revulsion against war began to be much more clearly expressed, and the pervasive attitudes of pacifism and anti-war during the 1930s meant that the popular attitudes towards the beginning of the Second World War had none of the jingoism of 1914. In general, the years of the First World War accelerated the trends whereby the political and industrial organizations of working people moved towards the centre of public life. The Liberal Party split and the Labour Party after 1918 became the largest opposition grouping. Trade union organization grew rapidly and by 1920 the total in unions was 8.25 million, with 6.5 million affiliated to the Trades Union Congress.

The years from 1917 to the middle of 1920 were a period of insurgency which, however, never reached revolutionary proportions. There was a widespread, if often inchoate, sentiment that affairs could not go on in the old ways; that pre-1914 Britain had gone for ever; and that butchery on the battlefields must never happen again. One immediate populist feeling was of the large-scale wartime profiteering that had gone on with only the feeblest of checks. The most obvious sign of discontent and disillusionment was the widespread unrest in the factories and the mines. 1919 was the most difficult year of all the postwar years for the Government and the propertied classes. There was uncertainty about the reliability of the armed forces in the event of their being used against civilian strikers; the police strike, which led to three days looting in Liverpool, was inevitably regarded as more serious than in fact it was; and a very turbulent industrial scene presented potentially dangerous situations. The year began with expressions of increasing discontent among the military stationed in Britain, especially those in London and the South of England. Dozens of vehicles were commandeered and troops poured into London to express their grievances. It was an independent movement with almost no contact or support from the organized labour movement. In industry the first important struggle was the strike on Clydeside to shorten the working week. It lasted from 27 January to 11 February, and it came out of the mass activity of the shop stewards on Clydeside during the war. But this most important strike exhibited the weaknesses of the whole movement, for most of the strike leaders, including Willie Gallagher, deliberately kept aloof from 'politics'. The national officials of the main unions involved kept the strike isolated, and had exerted their influence and official power to prevent other centres from sympathetic action, and except in Belfast they were successful; the executive of the Engineers suspended their district officials on the Clyde.

The most important industrial problem centred upon the miners. There were over a million coalminers in Britain; they were the best organized group of workers although still with a considerable degree of regional independence; and they had a long tradition of struggle. At a conference in Southport on 14 January 1919 the Miners Federation agreed to demand an increase in wages of 30 per cent, a six-hour working day and the nationalization of the mines with some measure of workers' control. When the demands were rejected by the Government a national ballot showed a large majority in favour of industrial action and notices of a national strike were given towards the end of February. The other members of the Triple Alliance were also preparing their own demands; but not in concert with the miners. Coal, however, was of outstanding importance, and a national strike at this time could have had very far-reaching effects upon the industrial politics of the Labour movement. Of that everyone was agreed, and it was therefore of quite central significance for the Government, and the most important single test for Lloyd George, in this very difficult year. He triumphed, by a combination of toughness, very shrewd bargaining, and a deception that was evident to most except the miners' leaders.

As a study in political deceitfulness, skilfully timed, the destruction of the miner's power in 1919 is the classic case in modern British history. The outcome, at the beginning of the conflict, was not automatic or inexorable, and it was not historically inevitable that the miners should go down to total defeat. But so long as the workers' representatives believed that their political rulers were men of their word and would honour what were the firmest of pledges, their defeat became certain. The sequence of events is familiar.[11] The Government offered a Royal Commission, to be chaired by Sir John Sankey, and equal representation of labour with the employers or their spokesmen; and they promised to implement its findings, provided that there was no strike. At the same time it was carefully explained to the miners' leaders that the Government were prepared to use all the coercive powers at their disposal if the national strike went ahead without waiting for the Commission's report; Robert Smillie, the miners' president, in particular was much influenced by these threats. Strike notices were suspended until the Royal Commission made its interim report which it did on 20 March. The evidence to the Commission had been sensational. Official Government witnesses had disclosed the rampaging profits which the coal industry had made during the war; the inefficient organization of the industry and its chaotic structure were impressively documented; and the working and living conditions of the miners and their families provided vivid copy for the newspapers and journals, most of which carried extensive coverage of the Sankey

Commission's hearings. On 20 March an interim report was published which gave an increase of two shillings a shift to underground workers, a reduction in working hours from eight to seven and what amounted to a serious commitment to consider critically the removal of ownership from private hands. On the same day as the report appeared Bonar Law, for the Cabinet, stated in the House of Commons that the Government would accept the final recommendations of the Sankey Commission and the next day – 21 March 1919 – he provided in a letter to the secretary of the Miners Federation a pledge that 'the Government are prepared to carry out in the spirit and in the letter' whatever recommendations Sankey would make. So the miners withdrew their strike notice, and the government had won time: the most precious factor in a time of crisis. When the Sankey Commission finally reported, on 23 June there were four reports: from the chairman, which recommended nationalization; from the six Labour representatives, which also argued unequivocally for national ownership; from five on the employers' side, which opposed any change from private control; and from a sixth member, Sir Arthur Duckham, who provided his own scheme. There were some differences between the proposals of Sir John Sankey and the miners' representatives, but Sankey firmly argued for state control of the mines. It was now the Government's opportunity to implement 'in the spirit and in the letter' the majority view of the Royal Commission. The Government, of course, had no intention of taking the mines out of private hands; and the intensive campaign, both public and in the corridors of Whitehall, to support the continued private ownership of the mines, contributed its share to the natural objections expressed by the whole business community, and its government at Westminster. The Government delayed a response and in the interim began to engage on a series of actions, from what in the later twentieth century would be called the department of dirty tricks. On 9 July the Government decided to raise the price of coal by six shillings a ton, the expectation being that it would help turn public opinion against the miners. Then the Coal Controller issued a quite unjustified order prohibiting any increase in piece rates in

[45]

excess of 10 per cent while negotiations about the new seven-hour day were under consideration. In the Yorkshire coalfield this led to a bitter strike of four weeks' duration, from the middle of July to mid-August. Troops went into the coalfield and naval ratings manned the pumps.

During this whole period, from the time of the Royal Commission's final reports on 23 June to the third week in August the government did nothing, while the press campaign against nationalization continued its furious way. Nor did the Miners Federation attempt in any serious or concerted way to continue the momentum of support which had undoubtedly built up as a result of the Sankey Commission's revelations. The Parliamentary Labour Party, led by J. R. Clynes and William Adamson, was weak and ineffective and, as has been usual throughout the twentieth century, there was no serious co-ordination of an attack upon the Government's handling of industrial matters. When Lloyd George, on 18 August, announced that the government would not accept nationalization, one of the arguments he used was to point to the Yorkshire strike as evidence that nationalization would not bring industrial harmony. The Government's own schemes were soon forgotten, and the Miners Federation found themselves in a situation less favourable to militant action than in the earlier months of the year, although contemporary evidence suggests that it was the leadership rather than the working miners who felt they could not go forward with strike action. For the present, the Federation leaders recommended constitutional agitation and launched a major campaign 'Mines for the Nation'. They were too late, and public opinion outside the mining areas was now concerned with other matters.

The Government had won, and they had won the most important issue of 1919, or, it can be argued, of the postwar years. If the mines had been nationalized in the aftermath of the war, the most reactionary group of property owners within the business community would have been broken up; and there would have been a corresponding increase in the political power of labour. The General Strike would probably not have taken place when it did, and the miners' union, the most cohesive organization within the trade union movement, would not have been paralysed for the next ten years as happened after 1926. It would not have brought socialism, or anything approaching a socialist commonwealth because the political leadership was too strongly labourist; but the victory of the miners in 1919 might have helped to make Britain a more civilized society. The employers would have had to be more reasonable, and what might have come about was an earlier and no doubt partial version of the Swedish middle road.

These are large speculations, but what is not conjecture is the aftermath of Lloyd George's victory over the miners in 1919. That he and his Conservative colleagues had to lie and prevaricate was an accepted part of the politics of a class society; just as was the deployment of the coercive powers of the state in ruthless ways when the situation was deemed to require the use of force. The Labour movement went on to win several battles: the railway strike of the autumn of 1919, and more impressive, the mobilization of a large part of working-class opinion against military intervention in the Soviet regime. But these were battles won in a war which, with the miners' defeat, was always going the way of the strongest; and when unemployment began to grow rapidly from the spring of 1921 – and to remain above the million mark for the rest of the interwar years – the trade union movement could only remain on the defensive and fight their piecemeal struggles. The reorganization of the Trades Union Congress and the establishment of the General Council, in place of the old Parliamentary Committee, was intended to help overcome the sectionalism of trade union action, but the crucial matter was the political composition of the General Council.

The years of the early 1920s were much disturbed, both in domestic politics and in the international situation. The general election of 1922 confirmed the Labour Party as the only serious opposition. Labour's parliamentary representation rose from 75 to 142, and Ramsay MacDonald was elected parliamentary leader, with the help of the Clydeside group, a decision they quickly regretted. In November 1923

Baldwin went to the polls and Labour now secured 192 seats with the Asquithian Liberals just behind with 157. Together they had a majority over the Tories' 258, and early in 1924 the first Labour Government – a minority one, of course – took office. It lasted less than a year and was hardly a success story, especially in the way MacDonald fought the 1924 election. The emphasis now shifted to the industrial front. The General Council of the TUC had a temporary leftish grouping of some considerable power, and the central issue was once again coal. The return to the Gold Standard in 1925 much exacerbated the problems of British exporters, including coal, and the coal-owners decided – it was on their part an automatic response to difficult times – upon heavy cuts in their wages bills. The miners stood firm, and the General Council backed them, and in the famous incident of 'Red Friday' the miners won a nine months' reprieve.

It was only an interval in the struggle. The Government and the mine-owners assumed that the conflict would be resumed, and they made their preparations accordingly; matched by indecision, inaction and false hopes on the worker's side. When the General Strike began on 3 May 1926, the General Council of the TUC, which in the intervening months had shifted in political complexion to the right, entered upon the struggle with reluctance from the outset. The strike was solid throughout the country, although by no means were all workers involved in the first week. Information poured into Transport House, the headquarters of the General Council, emphasizing the enthusiasm, dedication and commitment throughout the country. On Monday morning, 10 May, the General Council addressed a statement to the whole movement. It ended: 'The General Council's message at the opening of the second week is: "Stand Firm, Be Loyal to Instructions and Trust Your Leaders"'; and the Council took steps to call out on strike its first reserves – the remaining engineers and shipbuilders still at work. Within twenty-four hours the Council had decided to sue for peace and call off the strike; and on what basis? Here was a general strike which was increasingly paralysing the country. There was no break in the ranks. There were no negotiations either with the mine-owners or more importantly with the Government. All there was on the table was correspondence between the General Council and Sir Herbert Samuel who had put forward certain proposals on the basis of which the strike could be called off; the coal subsidy renewed 'for a reasonable time' while negotiations got under way. Samuel, however, as he carefully informed the General Council, had no official backing for his propositions; but it was on the basis of the Samuel proposals that the General Council asked for a meeting with the Prime Minister in order to inform him that the strike was to be terminated forthwith. This was on the morning of Wednesday 12 May and it was announced in the noon bulletin of the BBC.

The official record of the meeting between members of the General Council and seven ministers headed by Stanley Baldwin, the Prime Minister, makes incredible reading. The Government side gave no guarantees whatsoever in respect of the miners or the strikers in general; but they were not asked for. The General Council made no conditions at all. Those who spoke for them were frightened sheep; only Bevin uttered a bleat but not of any consequence. What most of the General Council had been working for, namely the end of the strike, was all that concerned them. The miners had already, on 11 May, firmly rejected the Samuel proposals; there was no attempt to convene a recall conference of all the trade unions on strike in order to explain the General Council's decision; the leading members of the Council had one aim, and one aim only, regardless of the consequences. It was to bring the General Strike to an end as quickly as possible; and the question is why?

There were some devious characters among the members of the General Council, none more so than J. H. Thomas, but what was common to all was their labourist philosophy which denied a basic class conflict in society and which assumed that reasonableness would always be met with reasonableness. Most of the General Council actually believed that Stanley Baldwin was an honest man, and not a Conservative politician subject to unrelenting pressure from vested interests in politics and business. There were many leading Tories at the time who were fully aware of how unpleasant most of the mine-owners were, and how impervious their minds were to reasonable arguments and suggestions. But when the lines were drawn, as in this strike, personal and political likes and dislikes were irrelevant. This was not something the General Council, individually or collectively, understood. For them there was a metaphysical entity known as the national interest in which all men of goodwill were involved. As Ernest Bevin said to Baldwin at the interview when the decision to terminate the strike was announced: 'I really felt in the event of our taking the lead in assuring you that we were going to play the game and put our people back, that it was going to be free and unfettered negotiations with the parties very speedily'. The trouble was that the mine-owners were unaccustomed to playing the game in Bevin's sense, and indeed it was not an image that would have come readily to their minds. So after the strike was called off, there was widespread victimization – the railway companies were particularly vicious – and the miners struggled on, for another six months, and went back defeated. The shock troops of the movement had once again been outmanoeuvred, and this time they were devastated.[12]

We have, then, two crucial episodes in the decade after the end of the First World War: the failure of the miners in 1919, largely the result of Government chicanery and double-dealing playing successfully upon the miners' leaders naïvety and trust; and the betrayal of the General Strike by the leaders of the trade union movement. Had the General Strike continued for another two or three weeks – and this assumes the leadership would have stood firm – the terms on which settlement would have been reached would obviously have been much more favourable to trade unionists as a whole, and to the miners in particular; and again, as with 1919, while nothing fundamental would have been changed, it would have given strength and courage to the movement as a whole, and helped to shift to some degree the balance of power away from the propertied groups. But this was also a problem for the General Council. In the years down to 1926 the struggle between themselves and the left, including the

Communists, had been unremitting; and while the block vote could in almost all cases be relied on, a victory in a general strike would undoubtedly have strengthened the left. It was a consideration that must be taken into account when assessing the motivations of the trade union leaders in May 1926.

Intervention by the political leaders of the movement in the events of 1926 were distinctly marginal. J. H. Thomas was a leading figure both at Westminster and in the General Council; and in general the quality of the political leadership of the Labour movement was mediocre. The first Labour Government of 1924 – a minority government – had illustrated the ineptness and weaknesses of the Labour leadership. There was a desperate insistence that Labour would work in the 'national interest', which meant, of course, that working-class concerns would not be given precedence; there was MacDonald's pathetic insistence upon the wearing of full ceremonial dress; J. H. Thomas' crude support for the Empire;[13] the use of all the methods previously employed against strikes and the strikers, including the threatened application of the Emergency Powers Act against a transport strike in London; and the continuation of the previous Conservative Government's defence policy, which included the building of five cruisers and two destroyers for the Navy and now implemented 'in view of the serious unemployment'. The thoroughly incompetent way in which Ramsay MacDonald handled the Zinoviev letter forgery rounded off less than a year's Labour Government which made it abundantly clear to even averagely well-informed observers that the propertied classes had nothing to fear from any administration headed by MacDonald and with a Chancellor of the Exchequer as inflexible a liberal as Philip Snowden. By 1926 the hopes of a new kind of postwar world had disappeared. It was not only that the British economy was failing to adapt to the changed conditions of the world economy, with the result that unemployment was endemic through all the interwar years, but the opportunities for what at best could only have been a partial restructuring of the social framework of society had also been wholly frustrated by the infirmity of purpose and the lack of serious comprehension

[51]

concerning the nature and character of bourgeois society on the part of the Labour and trade union leadership. The ordinary members of the Labour Party, and in particular the committed socialists, worked with the dedication and self-sacrifice that had always been exhibited by those at local and regional level; and it was their devotion to the cause that kept the Labour Party expanding its influence throughout the 1920s in spite of the craven and fumbling direction from above.

There was a left in these years as there had always been. In the federation which the Labour Party comprised, the Independent Labour Party was still the main agitational grouping, although the establishment of individual membership and constituency parties under the new constitution of 1918 was gradually to diminish the role of the ILP over the years. The ILP lost some of its left to the newly established Communist Party, but it still had an important working-class constituency, a lively press and some well-known and much respected militants. In H. N. Brailsford it had the outstanding socialist journalist of the interwar period. But by the end of the 1920s its internal dynamic was weakening, and its failure to develop factory groups, and fractions in unions, meant that it was going to lose out to the Communist Party. By the time the second minority Labour Government came to office in 1929 the number of ILP members of parliament who were still prepared to defer to the political discipline of the ILP's National Council had shrunk to a small minority of those who were still nominally members and when the ILP disaffiliated itself from the Labour Party in 1932, it immediately marginalized itself into political insignificance. The other main group on the left, the Communist Party, established in 1920, had a mixed history in the interwar years. It was originally a coming together of a number of separate strands on the left – the Socialist Labour Party, the British Socialist Party, the Guild Communists, a left group from the ILP and smaller miscellaneous groups of industrial workers and shop stewards with syndicalist tendencies. The Communist Party was much handicapped by the absence of a revolutionary tradition of any significance in Britain, and the weakness of a

Marxist culture; even more, since the Communist Party was affiliated from the beginning to the Communist International, there were and always have been serious problems in the relations between the party and the policies of the Comintern and in general of the Soviet Union. Its unswerving devotion to the political line of Moscow was to present serious problems and difficulties at different periods in its history. Down to 1926 the Communist Party was a few thousand in membership and still struggling to find its identity. It was lively and active if often unsure in its tactics; and it continued the bitter sectarianism which was already developing before 1914 against those it believed were betraying the cause. At the national level in these years the Communist Party was less influential than has often been supposed.[14]

4
The 1930s

The General Strike of 1926 is most commonly described in textbooks, and certainly remembered by the collective memory of the Labour movement, as an example of betrayal by the General Council (true) and as a magnificent illustration of working-class courage and endurance (also true). What is usually ignored, or at least played down, is the bitter fact that the defeat of the miners was total, and that the bargaining power of the Miners Federation was broken for more than a decade and not effectively recovered until the years of the Second World War. The implications of the collapse of the miners for the whole trade union movement were far-reaching. This most militant and best organized section of working people now largely disappeared from the common struggle; their collective voice was no longer heard as in the past; and against the background of an economy soon to be overcome by the great crisis of 1929 and the subsequent Depression, the forces of conservatism within the trade union movement had little difficulty in asserting their authority. Walter Citrine (1887–1983), the youngish general secretary of the TUC, and Ernest Bevin (1881–1951) were to emerge in the early 1930s as the dominant figures in the movement, and both were inclined quite firmly towards accommodation with the employers. It must be recalled that the greater part of the trade union movement had never been syndicalist – wage militancy is a different phenomenon – and certainly this was true of the trade union leadership. Citrine helped to draft the relevant sections of the presidential address given by George Hicks at the 1927 TUC which argued for 'effective machinery of joint consultation between the representative organizations entitled to speak for industry as a whole'. The appeal was answered by Sir Alfred Mond in the name of a number of industrialists, and while what became known as the Mond–Turner talks foundered in the growing economic crisis, both Citrine and Bevin defended the basic principles involved; that industrial problems were best dealt with by the two sides of industry, assisted by certain departments within the state apparatus, rather than by the politicians and their parties. As noted above, corporate bias had always been exhibited in some areas of British industry from the decline of Chartism on, although it was never pervasive through the economy in the nineteenth century, and it took on particular and often peculiar forms. Naturally, with growing organized strength on both sides of industry, and the developing problems of Britain in a highly competitive world economy, corporate bias displayed more sophisticated forms in the interwar years and the post-1945 decades; and, it must be emphasized, these developments affected not only the trade union movement but just as much the politics of Labour.

The immediate political consequences of the defeat of the miners and the earlier collapse of the General Strike were predictable. It had nearly always been the case that when industrial struggle failed, the working people turned to the ballot box. Before 1914 this had been almost entirely at the municipal level, but after the electoral reforms of 1918, as a number of commentators have argued, national voting for the first time came to be more representative of working-class opinion than ever before; although there were still a number of important anomalies in matters such as plural voting and registration problems. The harsh terms of the miners' settlement, and the industrial defeat of 1926, accelerated the trend towards Labour which was already a feature of the decade, and the 1929 general election was followed by the second Labour minority Government. Labour won its largest vote of the decade, 8.4 million votes with 288 seats in the House of Commons. The Tories had a slightly higher vote at 8.7 million but with only 260 seats; and the Liberals trailed with 59 seats. The greatest Labour gains were in Lancashire and Greater London, but hitherto difficult areas for Labour, such as Birmingham and the West Midlands, also showed impressive results. The North–South divide outside the London region was quite marked, for in the whole of the South, the South-West and the West of England Labour won only thirteen seats out of a total of ninety-four.

The political history of the second Labour Government was a history of unrelieved incompetence. There were a few – a very few – minor improvements in some social security benefits; but Snowden, again Chancellor of the Exchequer, was an unreconstructed nineteenth-century liberal in financial affairs, and inflexible to the point of stupidity. Mac-Donald was weak and vacillating, and the government drifted along to disaster, and was finally overcome by the financial crisis of the summer of 1931. Ramsay MacDonald, Snowden, J. H. Thomas and a few nonentities cut and ran, into a National Government dominated by Stanley Baldwin and the Tory Party. The general election which followed was disgraceful even by British twentieth-century standards, with the former Labour leaders' vigorous support of Tory scaremongering, and it produced a devastating defeat for Labour whose representation in the Commons was now reduced to just under fifty. Ramsay MacDonald – the 'boneless wonder' as he was not inaccurately described by Churchill – remained prime minister in what everyone knew was a Conservative government masquerading under the title of 'National'. Neville Chamberlain was the Chancellor of the Exchequer, and Baldwin the dominant political figure.[1]

The crisis of 1931, while not leading to any fundamental change in the direction of policy, was nevertheless in some ways a turning point for the Labour movement. Now the political situation looked different, and within the context of the shameless election campaign engineered by the Tories,

and the threatening international order against the background of world economic crisis, it was different.
'MacDonaldism without MacDonald' as a description of the
Labour leadership of the 1930s is more than half the truth
but it is not quite the whole story. Miliband, whose phrase it
is, was specifically confining himself to the Labour leaders,
and he was wholly justified:[2] they exhibited the same
degrees of caution and pusillanimity as in the 1920s. When
we speak, however, of the Labour leadership of the 1930s we
are referring first and foremost to the National Council of
Labour: a body dominated by trade unionists. In 1921 the
National Joint Council had been formed with equal numbers
from the TUC, the executive of the Labour Party and the
Paliamentary Labour Party. During the 1920s the National
Joint Council never played a prominent part in decision
making; but after the catastrophic electoral defeat of 1931 the
Trades Union Congress, through its General Council, circulated a memorandum proposing changes in the structure and
functions of the Joint Council. The unions were allocated
seven seats as against three each for the executive of the
Labour Party and the Parliamentary Labour Party. It was
renamed the National Council of Labour in 1934 and
throughout the decade exercised the dominant role in policy
making, and whatever decisions the National Council of
Labour came to they were not going to be overturned by
either of the other parties to the Council. The power relations
between the Labour Party – including the Parliamentary
Labour Party – and the trade union movement had always
varied within a fairly limited spectrum; it was, of course,
partly a matter of personalities and who controlled which
union, and partly the context within which decisions were
taken. In the 1920s the demarcation was less clear-cut and
decisive than it became in the decade which followed; but
after 1931 the trade union command of the National Council
of Labour and the block vote at annual conference – largely
within the control of the two big general unions – meant that
no major decision could be taken against the expressed
wishes of Bevin, Citrine and their allies. The political weakness of the Parliamentary Labour Party after the defeat of

[57]

1931 obviously encouraged the power of the trade union leaders and reinforced the conservatism of the post-1926 years.

There are, however, some qualifications that need to be made. The crisis of 1931 had profoundly disturbed the complacency which had affected large sections of the Labour movement concerning the ease with which radical change could be introduced; and the Labour intellectuals in particular were forced to reconsider their essentially liberal assumptions about the nature of political power. Even such a moderate socialist as R. H. Tawney felt it necessary to emphasize that the attempt to implement a socialist programme would be a 'pretty desperate business', to be met with 'determined resistance' by every section of the privileged classes; and the political position of the newly established Socialist League (1932), in the words of Stafford Cripps, was that in defence of their property rights the 'ruling class will go to almost any length to defeat Parliamentary action'. It was this sort of thinking that largely influenced the politics of the left in the first half of the 1930s, against the background of the worst economic crisis world capitalism had so far experienced.

These attitudes, and their political expression in books and pamphlets, have given rise to the widespread belief in later decades that the 1930s was a period of intense radicalization of the British, and other, Labour movements. In some respects the thesis can be sustained. The coming to power of Hitler in Germany in 1933; the Abyssinian campaign by Mussolini in 1935; above all the civil war in Spain which began in the summer of 1936; contributed greatly to the enhancement of radical political consciousness. The contrast, accepted by millions, between the apparent successes of planning in Soviet Russia and the wastefulness and desolation of the capitalist world was an additional and often quite crucial factor in the growth of left-wing movements. In Britain there were three social groups that were especially affected by the politics of the decade. The first was the Jewish community. The most important influence upon them was naturally the German Government with its policies of anti-Semitism; but the growth of a home-made Fascist movement with Oswald Mosley as its leader heightened the radical political consciousness that had always been a minority trend among the Jewish population, who were still mainly first or second generation immigrants. It was a radicalization, it should be noted, that affected not only the Jewish working class – the main target for anti-Semitic violence by Mosley's Fascists – but also sections of the middle class, businessmen as well as intellectuals. The last were especially important, although never as dominant in left-wing movements as in New York. The second group to be radicalized were the students, a phenomenon common to the United States but not to Continental Europe. The three main centres of student radicalization were Oxford, Cambridge and London Universities, especially the London School of Economics; and among other consequences this represented the first beginnings of a Marxist culture which went beyond the categories established by the working-class auto-didacts of the Plebs League, the Central Labour College and the National Council of Labour Colleges whose own importance is not in question.

The third social grouping radicalized by the events of the 1930s were certain sections of the working people, the most important of the three social categories being considered. It is not always easy to be precise about which parts of the working class were being politically radicalized as against acquiring a trade union consciousness, the result of the spread of union organization to hitherto unorganized groups. Metal workers all over western Europe in the first half of the twentieth century were to be found in the forefront of the politically conscious workers: the result of a changing labour process into mass-production technology which encouraged a continuing militancy; and new industries, such as automobile manufacturing, were to lead to unionization on a large scale, although in many countries including Britain this did not occur until after the Second World War. In Britain, the Communist Party was the most important single factor in the growth of militancy at the point of production and the politicization of many trade-union-conscious workers; but it was not until the 1930s that the Communist Party began to make a serious and more lasting impact upon the trade union movement in general.

The conscious indoctrination of a class attitude among industrial workers really began with the Socialist Labour Party after 1903, and the Communist Party inherited its traditions, now mixed with those being accepted from Moscow. The Independent Labour Party had always engaged in general political activity, but did not have factory groups, and the Socialist League, established in 1932, was a movement largely of intellectuals and Labour Party activists. After its foundation in 1920 the Communist Party seriously tried to build a revolutionary party on an industrial basis – part of the central creed of the early Congresses of the Communist International – but inexperience within a pervasive labourist tradition meant that little progress was made. In the General Strike the influence of the Communist Party was important in certain areas but not over the country as a whole – its leading political figures were all in gaol – and the general impact of the Communist Party on events in 1926 has often been much exaggerated, not least by those who argue the 'missed' revolutionary opportunities of 1926. The influence of the Communist Party and the associated Minority movement was in fact limited in the 1920s, and its influence sharply declined with the acceptance of the 'social-Fascist' line developed at length at the Sixth World Congress of the Communist International.[3] At the beginning of the 1930s the Communist Party was still enmeshed within the sectarian stupidities of the 'Class Against Class' line; and at a time when the economic crisis was steadily worsening through 1930 and 1931, continued sectarianism eroded the influence of the Party. The basic assumption of the world Communist movement was that the economic collapse of capitalism was irreversible, and that this would inevitably encourage a revolutionary upsurge the world over. Whatever happened or was likely to happen elsewhere, this was never a possibility in Britain; Maynard Keynes said of a volume by von Hayek that it was an example 'of how, starting with a mistake, a remorseless logician can end up in Bedlam' and this could equally be applied to some at least of the theoretical writings at this time of Rajni Palme Dutt, the British Communist Party's outstanding theoretician. It has been a very common error of vulgar Marxism to assume that there is a simple and direct relationship between material conditions and social consciousness; and the blind faith with which the Communist parties followed the Moscow line produced a situation in Britain in which the Communist Party was at its lowest ebb, at a time when unemployment was rising to unprecedented levels. By the beginning of the 1930s the Communist Party had a total membership of between three and four thousand; and according to the report given to the 1932 Battersea Congress their total was now 5,400 of whom 60 per cent were unemployed. The Party's influence in the trade union movement had shrunk to quite negligible proportions.

The British Communist Party did not, however, remain in this situation of political impotence. It had never wholly lost touch with social reality, and it contained within its membership a number of outstanding personalities. Indeed, it is probably true to say that during the interwar years the British Communist Party collected within its ranks the most dedicated, the most disciplined and the most effective group of militants that the Labour movement in Britain has ever seen working together. Why they did not achieve more than the record shows is a quite central question to which at least some answers will be suggested later. But miners' leader Arthur Horner was already unwilling to follow the social-Fascist line in 1930 in trade union work; and others, like Wal Hannington, continued their independent activity on behalf of the unemployed. More significant was the successful case that Harry Pollitt made at the end of 1931, that the Comintern's attitude towards trade unions in Britain must change; and what became known as the 'January' resolution accepted the need for new approaches to trade union work, including work within the 'reformist' trade unions (which meant the existing unions). While there was quite strong opposition within the British Party, including that of Palme Dutt, the line of work did change, especially in the direction of the encouragement of rank and file movements; and these were to be important in the coming years.[4] The Party was, it must be emphasized, an organization whose leaders and rank and file were almost wholly working people, most of whom had come to politics through the trade union movement. Their own common sense began to reassert itself, and the changing political line of the Comintern, much accelerated after the victory of the Nazis in Germany, permitted a fresh turn towards the mass organizations of the Labour movement. The Communist Party never overcame the full consequences of the disastrous years between 1928 and 1932, and the mistrust and bad faith engendered were never forgotten. In spite of the inspiration which it provided in the second half of the 1930s and the energy it imparted to the whole movement, the Communist Party was a prisoner of its past as well as of its continuing acceptance of Moscow directives. But without the Communist Party the history of the 1930s, from about 1933 to 1939, would have been very different. They provided the dynamic behind the organization of the four national hunger marches, much of the opposition to Mosley and the Fascist movement, and a great deal of the extraordinary efforts that went to support Republican Spain in the civil war, including the recruitment of a high proportion of the British section of the International Brigade from among Communist Party members. Work on the factory floor and the encouragement of rank and file movements in transport, printing offices and aircraft factories were the most solid achievements of these years; with metal workers generally providing the largest group of Party members and sympathizers. In the coalfields Communist influence was surprisingly regionalized: strong in South Wales and parts of Scotland, but much more patchy elsewhere. By 1939 the Party had about 20,000 members and their political and social influence was considerably greater than these figures would immediately suggest.[5]

This decade of the 1930s cannot be assessed without reference to the extraordinary influence of Soviet Russia upon political attitudes in the Western-type democracies. In Britain, after the ending of the wars of intervention against the young Soviet Republic, the greater part of the Labour movement was not noticeably concerned with internal Russian affairs during the 1920s. It was the coincidence in time between the beginning of the world economic crisis at the end of the 1920s and the launching of the first Five Year Plan that brought about a much deeper interest in contemporary Russia. As the dole queues lengthened, and families became grimly familiar with the problems of living without work, on security benefits that were tightly means tested, it was not at all extraordinary that large numbers of working people and intellectuals should begin to look upon the Soviet Union with a new understanding and sympathy. A complete list of books and pamphlets favourable to the Soviet Union published throughout the decade would be a very long one, while the published evidence to the contrary, except in the columns of the right-wing press, was not very impressive. The most important work was undoubtedly W. H. Chamberlain's *Russia's Iron Age*, which appeared in 1934, the year he left the Soviet Union after a stay of twelve years as correspondent of the *Christian Science Monitor*. No other critical volume in the English language and written by an outside observer was as effective as *Russia's Iron Age*, but its circulation in Britain was limited, and it had to be put alongside the Webbs' *Soviet Communism, A New Civilisation?* first published in 1935, with the question mark removed for the second edition of 1937.

One of the important aspects of the pro-Soviet attitudes of the 1930s was the image that became accepted in the West of Joseph Stalin. Walter Citrine, for example, whose book *I Search for Truth in Russia*, provided a critical account of the Soviet Union which was highly sceptical of the processes of democracy, nevertheless gave a not unflattering account of Stalin himself. There were few published interviews with Stalin, but the general impression he made was that of a highly controlled, intelligent leader, in sharp contrast with both Hitler and Mussolini. One of the most remarkable assessments of Stalin was published in John Gunther's *Inside Europe*, a book which had a phenomenal sale in Britain and America. Gunther gave a blistering analysis of both Nazism and Fascism, and he did not slur over the harsh facts of the 'Iron Age' in the years of early collectivization in Russia. But his commentary on Stalin, taken from the first edition, reads in part:

Let no one think that Stalin is a thug. It would be idle to pretend that he could take a chair in fine arts at Harvard; nevertheless his learning is both broad and deep, especially in philosophy and history . . .

Nor are his manners bad. He sees visitors only very rarely, but one and all they report his soberness, his respectful attention to their questions, his attempt to put them at their ease . . . He is the only dictator who is *serene*.

The italics were Gunther's. By the middle of the decade, however, it was foreign policy that was the most important factor in the shift of public opinion towards a pro-Soviet position. The public statements of Litvinov and other Soviet diplomats and leaders were in striking contrast with the speeches and actions of the National Government in Britain. The deal with Italy over Abyssinia, the policies towards the Spanish Republic when the military began the civil war, and later Munich, all convinced the greater part of the Labour movement that the Conservatives were not to be trusted. Whatever qualifications historians in recent years have placed upon the motivations of Chamberlain and Halifax, many contemporaries well outside the left were equally convinced that what became known as 'appeasement' was to be equated with pro-Fascist attitudes. What was sharply revealed to the majority of the rank and file activists of the British Labour movement was the inability of the ruling groups to provide employment at home – there were still a million unemployed in the peak growth year of 1937 – as well as their pursuit of a foreign policy that was a betrayal of the interests of peace. The Soviet Union stood in stark contrast, and it was clearly understood that without the Soviet Union there could be no solid front of opposition to international Fascism.

It was the years of the trials, mostly of the old Bolsheviks, that might have begun a more questioning debate concerning the nature and character of Soviet society, but with exceptions that will be remarked on, it did not take place. And the main reason was the rapidly worsening inter national edi . The litical trials , just minds of socialists in the West. The British Government backed non-intervention, which meant a free hand for Italy and Germany; the Soviet Union gave tangible aid to the Republican government. The issues were understood in simple, compelling terms, and while there was disquiet among many about the trials, matters of peace and war were of overriding importance. Bukharin, following the last of the major open trials, was shot on 15 March 1938, three days after the Germans marched into Austria. His appeal to the world, made in a coded last speech to the court, was drowned by the noise of the war machines preparing for action.

The Moscow trials were a gigantic confidence trick; a frame-up of extraordinary ingenuity and invention. The problem for the historian is to try to explain the reactions of contemporaries without falling into apologetics, and seriously to analyse the now more commonly accepted argument that the left and their liberal allies were the naïve dupes of Moscow propaganda. The most important reason has been suggested. It was stated succinctly in 1941 by Louis Fischer, one of the great American journalists of these years:

> Why, instead of holding my tongue, did I not come out in 1937 or 1938 as a critic of the Soviet regime? It is not so easy to throw away the vision to which one has been attached for fifteen years. Moreover, the Soviet government's foreign policy was still effectively anti-appeasement and anti-fascist, much more so than England's or France's or America's. It helped China with arms to fight Japanese aggression. It helped Spain to fight Nazis and Mussolini. It encouraged Czechoslovakia to stand firm against Hitler. I did not know how long it would last. But while it lasted, I hesitated to throw stones in public. Even now I think I was right.

But this is not the whole of the answer. An aspect of the trials which greatly misled contemporaries was the volume of testimony which insisted upon the correctness of the judicial procedures, the good health of the defendants, and the openness of their testimony. There were no signs of physical torture; Radek joked with the court, and Bukharin argued with, and rejected, a number of the accusations put to him by the Public Prosecutor. But no one – except Krestinsky in the last trial, and he retracted the following day – spoke a word which suggested the evidence was faked. A careful analysis of the verbatim record was a different matter, as Voigt and others argued. Apart from the contemporary writing on the trials, when Joseph E. Davies, who was American Ambassador to Moscow from 1936 to 1938, published his *Mission to Moscow* in 1942, it was revealed that Davies had been convinced of the guilt of the accused and that he had been sending cables back to Washington to that effect. Davies, it should be added, was a lawyer and a businessman, and as he makes clear he was in daily contact with the American newspaperman who were covering the trials.

It must not be thought, however, that there was no critical response to the trials in Britain. The most remarkable analysis was by the conservative journalist F. A. Voigt, the *Manchester Guardian's* diplomatic correspondent, in a six-page footnote at the end of his *Unto Caesar*, published in 1938. The *Manchester Guardian* itself, of all the liberal and radical newspapers, was the most cogent and compelling in its scepticism; and its letter columns were filled with a wide-ranging selection of the arguments on both sides, including a remarkable series of letters from European social-democrats and Russian émigrés, mostly writing from Paris addresses. The Labour Party published an English version of Friedrich Adler's *The Witchcraft Trials in Moscow*, and it was given publicity, among other places, in the *New Statesman* by Leonard Woolf. H. N. Brailsford consistently regretted and sharply criticized the trials. The most persistent sceptic among the Labour movement journalists was Emrys Hughes, editor of the Scottish *Forward*, who flatly refused to believe that the confessions were genuine and who conducted a principled editorial policy throughout, opening his letter columns to both sides. The *New Statesman* was probing in its appraisal, and no one who read its columns carefully could remain without doubts and anxieties. On the other side, *Left News*, the widely circulated monthly journal of the Left Book Club – itself a major publishing event of these years – was almost completely dominated in its writings on the Moscow trials by Ivor Montagu, a highly persuasive and sophisticated apologist, John Strachey and Pat Sloan, the last being among the most assiduous of all pro-Soviet letter writers to the national press.

It cannot be denied that the response to the Moscow trials was less critical in Britain than it was in either France or the United States. For one thing, there was no Trotskyist movement of any significance in Britain, and the few Trotskyists there were mostly engaged in dogmatic disputation amongst themselves. In part at least, the British situation reflected the domination of the labourist ethos, and the absence of a serious tradition of Marxist culture. The practical common sense of most activists in the British movement could hold two discordant themes in their minds, without apparent contradiction and without any obvious intellectual tension. One was a broad scepticism in general about democracy in the Soviet Union – a scepticism barely articulated at the time except by a minority of the leadership such as Citrine, Bevin and some parliamentarians – and the other was a vision of the absence of unemployment, of rising living standards and the fierce opposition in foreign policy to Fascism. In the longer run, as the facts concerning the nature of certain parts of Soviet society became authenticated without qualification, the 'broad scepticism' about the failure of internal democracy became confirmed; and the continuing revelations of Stalinism in the years after the Second World War were to exercise a profound effect upon beliefs in the nature of socialism itself.

The choice before the Labour Party in the 1930s was never between moderation and caution, on the one hand, and a revolutionary programme on the other, although it was often presented by some of the contemporary left in these ways. In no meaningful analysis could the British situation be described as revolutionary, or potentially revolutionary, and those on the left who took this view were at fault in their analysis. Their mistake, of course, can be understood. Capitalism as a world system was in deep and serious crisis between 1929 and 1933, and the fact of crisis had penetrated social consciousness on a wide scale. But it was an elementary error to infer from economic crisis an automatic revolutionary response from those who were its victims. The contrary would seem to have been the case in most periods in the history of British labour. For the mass of the working people in the 1930s what the Labour Party had to do was to rehabilitate itself in terms of its collective capacity to govern; the Party could only do this if it was able to sustain a vigorous and continuous critique of Government policy and practice and at the same time offer what could be presented as a viable alternative. What was required was a massive shift towards Labour, and this never happened in the 1930s. In the long history of the evolution and development of a working-class party in Britain, there has always been a subtle and complicated interplay between unionization and political attitudes. In broad terms in the twentieth century, up to at least the end of the 1950s and in many areas later than that, the greater the unionization of an industry, town or region, the more likely has been the shift towards the Labour Party in voting terms. Moreover, the political working-class militant has almost always been a trade unionist, and the trade union was traditionally the school through which the young militant, most of whom at this time were male, first learned his political ideas. There were exceptions, of course, not least with the emergence of youth movements attached to militant groups of the left; but these were largely developments in the post-1950 period. There are some wider implications. There is nothing in England (until fairly recently one could have written mainland Britain) comparable with the appeal to the masses of anarchism in Catalonia, or republicanism in Ireland, or revolutionary ideas for sections of the Parisian workers. The post-1850 character of developing labourism in Britain was denuded of the social radicalism of the Owenite years, and political radicalism, as it developed in the second half of the nineteenth century, was built upon a fairly narrowly constructed set of ideas; it was largely the influence of trade unionism that began, slowly, to widen the political horizons of ordinary workers. There are two questions to be asked of the 1930s in order to discover the reasons for the uneven and partial recovery of the Labour movement from the catastrophe of 1931. The first relates to the quality of the political leadership being offered, and the second to the trade union history of the decade.

Labour's political history of the 1930s was for the most part uninspiring and certainly ineffective. The Parliamentary Party remained wedded to the constitutional struggle inside Westminster, and while the Labour Party in certain parts of the country, notably London, was at times more lively, the general tone of the movement was largely dictated by the national leadership. The immediate problem after 1931 was to rebuild the confidence of the Labour rank and file. A great deal of the energy of the first half of the decade went into the preparation and discussion of programmes and policies for a future Labour administration; and these were presented at successive annual conferences after 1932. Hugh Dalton was the key figure in the determination of economic and financial policy. He was a member of the crucial policy committee established by the executive committee at the end of 1931, and his ideas were embodied in the most important state-ment of a Labour programme that was published during the 1930s. This was *Practical Socialism for Britain*, written during 1934 and published in the spring of 1935. It was certainly not the most exciting book of the decade, and left-wing contem-poraries regarded it as a reformist document of no great significance. But Dalton was at the centre of the Labour Party in the 1930s and he was gathering around himself a group of young socialist intellectuals who were themselves to help determine the contours of policies when the Labour Party took office in 1945. The group included Hugh Gaitskell, Evan Durbin, Douglas Jay, Colin Clark, and Nicholas Davenport, and while the left may remember Harold Laski, G. D. H. Cole, William Mellor and John Strachey and the galaxy of Left Book Club writers, it was the Dalton–Gaitskell group who provided the ideas for 1945.

Ideas about the future, however, whatever their character in terms of the reformist/radical debate, were no substitute for action on contemporary problems; and what the Labour Party had to do in the 1930s was first to win back the working-class electorate of the late 1920s and then to expand and develop its political influence. The Labour victory in the London County Council elections of 1934 was an important advance; but there was no comparable achievement at the national level. The general election of 1935 came almost exactly four years after 1931; years of massive unemployment, although the economy had been moving up from the low point of 1932, the result mainly of protectionism and the agreements on foreign trade, the growth in the building sector and the development of the 'new' industries in the Midlands and the London region. Labour added just over one hundred seats to its 1931 figure. The total number of votes cast for Labour nearly reached the 1929 peak, but the electorate had increased by 2.5 million, and the turn-out on election day was 8 per cent down. The main Labour gains were in London, Scotland and Yorkshire. The centres of strength – which in terms of seats all fell short of 1929 – were still the coalfields and selected urban areas. Trade union MPs numbered 79 out of a total of 154, the miners remaining the largest group with 34. As in 1931 there was not a single Labour MP for any of the twelve Birmingham constituencies, and it was the county boroughs in England, outside the coalfields, most of the industrial North and London, that were the major areas of electoral weakness. The rural regions, almost everywhere, were well beyond the chances of a Labour victory. There was a fairly steady improvement in Labour's local election results over the whole decade; but again the geographical spread was uneven.

What Labour was failing to do in the 1930s was to continue to win over the very large numbers of manual workers, and even more their wives and daughters, who either voted for one of the other two major parties or were politically uncommitted. At the time, Harold Laski noted that the unemployed, outside the coalfields, voted in 1935 for the Tories; or, he might have added, 'did not vote at all'. Labour's upward trend of the 1920s had been broken, and it was this failure to overcome the disastrous consequences of 1931 that provided the major problem of the decade for Labour. In the 1930s the Labour Party was still, in the social composition of its leadership as well as in its rank and file, a working-class party. There was a middle-class Labour element at Westminster, and the period of the Left Book Club witnessed an increase in middle-class support for the Labour movement; but the national constitutency for the Labour Party was the working class, and their policy had above all else to be concerned with working-class hopes and aspirations.

The most serious social question was unemployment, and its associated consequences of poor housing, inadequate diet and above-average illness. The extent of unemployment was never fully revealed in official statistics, and long-term or short-term unemployment affected all sections of manual workers, with only obvious exceptions such as railwaymen, print workers and most municipal employees. Apart from the favoured groups, there was never full employment in the post-1945 sense, and even in the more prosperous years of the mid 1930s, seasonal fluctuations were common to many trades and industries. The TUC always insisted that the unemployed worker was the responsibility of his appropriate union, but many unemployed had never been union members; and for the rest the TUC advocated provision of social facilities. It was all half-hearted and wholly ineffectual. What was not lacking in vigour, however, was the denunciation by the Labour leadership of bodies outside the Labour Party who were engaged in agitation on behalf of the unemployed. The most important was the National Unemployed Workers' Movement, which organized national hunger marches to London on four occasions in the 1930s: 1930, 1932, 1934 and 1936. Not one of these marches was supported officially, and the local Labour Parties and Trades Councils were specifically instructed to offer no help. The reason was that the NUWM was led and organized by Communists although a number of left-wing Labour militants were always involved. Only in 1936 – to a lesser extent in 1934 – were the bans imposed widely disregarded. In the 1936 reception in Hyde Park, Attlee was among a number of leading personalities who spoke from one of the many platforms. The most extraordinary episode, which illuminated more clearly than any other the stupid, reactionary and politically self-destructive attitudes of the

Labour establishment, was the refusal to support the Jarrow march of October–November 1936. The march was organized by the town council (which in 1936 had just been won by Labour) and the sitting MP, Ellen Wilkinson. It was an all-party affair with the Conservative and Labour agents forming the advance guard who went ahead of the main body of marchers. The publicity the Jarrow march achieved was enormous; far greater than any of the NUWM marches. The TUC, the Labour Party National Executive and the National Council of Labour, all refused their formal support. The Labour Party met in conference at Edinburgh just after the march began and Ellen Wilkinson was refused support. But to show their compassion, the Executive decided to institute the first large-scale investigation the Labour Party had undertaken into the problems of unemployment; a Commission of Enquiry into the Depressed Areas.[6]

This failure of the Labour leadership to develop a continuous campaign against the major social evil of the decade was typical of Labour's general political attitudes. The Labour Party leadership took no part in any of the important political initiatives of this decade. In spite of the extraordinary passion evoked by the Spanish Civil War, the Labour Party never conducted a major campaign throughout the country on any of the issues involved, except for a desultory attempt after the 1937 annual conference. The decade is connected above all with the hunger marches, with the street battles against Mosley and his Fascists, and with Spain; and the energies unloosed around these issues, and the political commitment entered into, can at no point be credited to the Labour leaders. Only against appeasement is the record partially acceptable, and here, as with all else, the struggle was confined to Westminster. To characterize the Labour leadership as incompetent and ineffectual is not only a judgement of hindsight, it was precisely and exactly what was being pronounced at the time, by an increasing number of Labour activists as well as by non-Labour commentators.

The most obvious political characteristic of the 1930s was the way in which successive Conservative Governments were able to ignore, on all fundamental matters, the Labour

Party inside Westminster and the political and industrial movements outside. There were occasions when the Government had to submit to outraged public opinion – the retreat on the unemployment regulations in January–February 1935, or the resignation of Samuel Hoare after the disclosure of the negotiations with Laval in late 1936 – but the exceptions were few, and Government submission was never simply the result of Labour pressure alone. Conservative Governments in the 1930s went their own way, and the feebleness of the Labour opposition was a constant theme of political journalists and leader writers.

The crucial influence in the political decisions of the late 1930s, made in the name of the official Labour movement, belonged to the leading trade unionists of the period, and in particular to Ernest Bevin and Walter Citrine. They had allies among the Labour politicians at Westminster, but real power remained with the trade union leaders, and no major issue of the decade went against the wishes of Bevin and his colleagues in the TUC. Through their control of the block vote they dominated the annual conferences of both the TUC and the Labour Party; and above all, they always had a majority on the National Council of Labour. Their own record in the field of trade union recruitment and development was emphatically not a success story. The peak affiliation of trade unionists to the TUC was in the years 1919 and 1920, when around 6.5 million workers were represented. By the year of the General Strike this total had fallen to about 4.25 million, and following the defeat of the General Strike, the membership affiliated remained under 4 million from 1927 to 1935. Trade union numbers were moving slowly upwards after 1932, but while the total was just over 4 million in 1936, the 5-million mark was not passed until 1940, the first full year of war.

The failure of the trade union movement to initiate a forward movement was widely commented on at the time. The geographical shift in employment opportunities towards the Midlands and London and the South-East was not matched by a new vigour in union activity. There was nothing in Britain to set against the achievements of the

[73]

Congress of Industrial Organizations (CIO) in the United States or the French unions during the period of the Popular Front. The union leaders in Britain lacked imagination, inspiration and energy. Their minds were closed to the new possibilities that had opened up before them and in the case of Bevin and the majority of the General Council, anti-Communism was a stronger sentiment than anti-employer. It is true that the fastest growing unions were the two general unions; the Transport Workers of which Bevin was general secretary, and the General and Municipal Workers. But what was achieved was limited compared with the possibilities; and both unions had high turnovers of membership, and a hierarchical structure of organization which kept power firmly in the hands of full-time officials. The London busmen's rank and file movement, which had become a powerful body by the mid 1930s and which showed the potential of organization, was able to call a strike on the eve of the Coronation celebrations, for 1 May 1937. Communists and left-wing militants dominated the leadership of the busmen; and Bevin broke the strike after a month and expelled its leaders. This shattering of the London busmen's movement had repercussions far beyond London and its transport workers. A victory in the summer of 1937 would have given heart to the whole trade union movement. As it was, another failure, imposed once again by the trade union machine, further undermined confidence and encouraged the feelings of helplessness against the conservatism of the Labour establishment.[7]

It was to be the same story on the political front. The most difficult problem during the second half of the 1930s was the issue of rearmament. It was a matter of much complexity which has often been greatly simplified by commentators in recent decades. There was first the growth of anti-war and pacifist sentiment; not by any means synonymous. Both were a strong reaction against the butchery of the First World War, and both reached their peak influence in the mid 1930s. Egon Wertheimer, the German social democrat, in his interesting study of the British Labour Party first published in England in 1929, noted that the British people were deeply pacifist in their attitudes, but it was not until the later 1920s that the literature of anti-war really begun to appear in considerable volume and its organizational expression also began to develop from this time. On the pacifist side the Peace Pledge Union, not established until 1934, reached 100,000 members by 1936; and on the political anti-war side the first half of the 1930s saw a vigorous and rapidly growing movement against the private manufacture of arms and a growing consciousness of the evil practices of the arms dealers in encouraging wars. The sale of arms by post Second World War governments, partly to influence regional power conflicts, partly to assist balance of payments problems, would have been inconceivable to the Labour movement of the 1930s, regardless of their political tendencies. Political obscenity, they would all have argued, could go no further.

There was a paradox here. At the time when German Fascism was beginning to exhibit its aggressive, expansionist policies from the mid 1930s on, the anti-war movement and pacifist sentiment were at their peak. From 1936 the question of whether to support the rearmament programme of the Conservative Government was increasingly at the centre of Labour Party politics. It was the right wing of the Labour movement who were generally in favour of support; Dalton among the politicians and Bevin and Citrine for the trade unions. The issue was at the time often presented as separate from foreign policy, an argument which the left strongly resisted. The Parliamentary Party first abstained on the defence estimates in July 1937 and at the annual conference later in the year the Dalton line was overwhelmingly accepted. Henceforth the majority position was clear: support for rearmament while continuing opposition to the Government's foreign policy. The problem was that opposition to any part of the Government's policy was normally weak and indecisive.

The response of the left was vigorous but muddled. Aneurin Bevan offered the most coherent statement for the opposition view in his speech to the 1937 conference. He noted that a government with the majority it had in the House of Commons could not in any case be denied a rearmament programme. The Labour vote would have no consequence whatever, whichever way it was given. The question therefore was to enunciate a principled policy – a socialist policy – in a world in which the Fascist powers, in Europe and the Far East, were being appeased, that is assisted, by the attitudes and policies of Britain and France. The point that Bevan made was that the left would support without hesitation a rearmament programme provided it was part of a progressive foreign policy. It was an argument that was not developed in subsequent debates, and in later discussions it was never explained and clarified; but it was clearly the only basis on which political opposition to the Conservative Government's policies could be justified. The strength of the feeling that Chamberlain in particular was incapable of being trusted was well expressed by R. H. Tawney, a middle-of-the-road socialist and not one identified with the left at any time in his career. In a remarkable letter to the *Manchester Guardian* in March 1938 Tawney exemplified the anxieties and despondency which had overtaken those confronted with a government believed to be actively abetting the policies of international Fascism. Tawney's letter, spread over two columns, actually suggested that the Parliamentary Labour Party might serve the cause better by withdrawing *en bloc* from Parliament, and stumping the country with its opposition to the Government. 'Why,' wrote Tawney 'should we make and pay for armaments to carry out a policy precisely the opposite from that which our rulers put forward when they asked to be returned to power.'[8]

Aneurin Bevan, in his speech already mentioned, made a further point. He argued that the question of support, or not, for rearmament was inextricably involved with the more general problems of Labour tactics and strategy. People like himself had been for many years engaged in an endeavour to instil more militant attitudes into the Labour leadership, inside the Commons and outside. As explained above, on all the central issues of the 1930s the actions and activity of the Labour and trade union leadership could hardly be described as vigorous or inspiring. Rather the contrary. Their caution, concern for respectability, and apparent lack of awareness at the grim prospects of a world in which international Fascism seemed to move from one triumph to another, with the support of the British ruling classes, were the despair and desolation of many in Britain well beyond the traditional groups of the organized left. Attlee, for example, of all the leading figures in the Labour movement, was the only one to visit Republican Spain. Nye Bevan was highly conscious of these problems, and he saw the acceptance of the rearmament policy as further evidence of the leadership refusing to commit themselves to outright opposition to the hated government. In the same speech at the 1937 conference, Bevan elaborated:

> You cannot collaborate, you cannot accept the logic of collaboration on a first class issue like rearmament, and at the same time evade the implication of collaboration all along the line when the occasion demands it. Therefore, the Conference is not merely discussing foreign policy; it is discussing the spiritual and the physical independence of the working-class movement of this country. It has faced us in the House of Commons, and will face us in the months to come.

This speech by Aneurin Bevan could have provided the left with the basis for a coherent policy. But the debate which followed the 1937 conference did not extend and clarify the arguments the left were using. Two aspects in particular were played down or ignored. The first, and most important, ought to have been the insistence that opposition to rearmament by the Chamberlain Government was not a pacifist opposition, and that what the International Brigade were demonstrating in Spain – the willingness to take up arms against the Fascists – should have been at the centre of the whole debate as defined by the left. It was this failure to state the problem in a clear-cut way that led to much confusion, and a distinctly muffled understanding of the left's position. The Communist Party, for example, agreed with most of Bevan's approach; but they argued first and foremost for the peace front of Britain, France and the Soviet Union, and insisted that talk of an 'inevitable war' was defeatist. And this undoubtedly led to illusions about maintaining European peace, and the power of the ordinary people through their mass organizations in overcoming their own ruling class appeasers. The second aspect of the problem was Bevan's insistence upon the problem of 'independence' and here it was the trade union leaders – Bevan and Citrine in particular – who were especially sympathetic to co-operation both with industry and the Government. It was not that they were necessarily more inclined to collaboration than most of the Labour politicians, but during the years from 1926 they had more opportunity. Walter Citrine took a knighthood in 1935 and within a decade the British Labour movement, which previously had strong feelings about accepting honours from anyone, and above all from a Conservative Government, had come to accept the system which in theory they continued to denounce. Bevin and Citrine became increasingly close to Government circles as war approached and as the rearmament programme began to involve the trade union movement in general in the details of its development. What the political side did was to tighten its internal discipline against the accusations from the left that it was failing to encourage a serious movement of continuous protest against the policies of the Chamberlain Government. First the attempt to achieve a United Front on the left, and then the Popular Front agitation, led in the end to the expulsion of Stafford Cripps in the first half of 1939 and of half a dozen more who supported him – including Aneurin Bevan. There are reasonable arguments that can be adduced against the Popular Front tactic, or the way in which the left permitted themselves to be isolated from the mainstream of the movement; but what needs to be emphasized is that the Labour Party leadership had nothing to offer as an alternative save the injunction to take note of the parliamentary battles at Westminster and to prepare for the next general election. Subsequent analysis, it should be noted, has suggested that a general election in 1940 – assuming war had not come – would have given a third consecutive victory to the Tories. Before 1939 neither the trade union leaders nor the Labour politicians took serious measure of the grim and menacing international situation they found themselves in. They gave no hope or inspiration to their supporters, and were tough, uncompromising and energetic only when their own positions of power were threatened. They placated those who were their enemies, and discouraged their friends. Moreover, Attlee's leadership of the Labour Party was never secure after his election to office in late 1935, and the divisions and controversies about the leadership, widely publicized, helped to confirm their political weightlessness in the country at large.

It was, therefore, in keeping with the low morale of the ordinary party worker that the annual conference at Whitsuntide 1939 was the quietest, and the most listless, of any in the decade that had just passed. By the time this last peacetime Labour conference convened, the Spanish Civil War was over and Franco had been recognized by the British Government; Hitler had entered Prague; Italy had seized Albania; and Chamberlain had given his extraordinary guarantee to Poland while conducting desultory negotiations with the Soviet Union. This was the international background to the conference. The leadership had refused every initiative to build a firmer base of opposition to the Government, and they had expelled their main critics. By the time of the conference the platform had nothing to propose to their delegates except continued support for the rearmament programme and a policy document, *Labour's Immediate Programme*, in anticipation of the next year's general election. What was made certain was the domination by the leadership over their own delegates and members. The annual conference of the Labour League of Youth had already been cancelled and this was confirmed by the conference. As Dalton wrote in his memoirs after Cripps' expulsion at the beginning of 1939: 'we were in a fight to a finish.'[9] Stirring words, which Dalton never used about the Conservative governments of these years. But Dalton was right; they fought and they won; and the conference, with the block vote of the major unions, acquiesced. The demoralization among the delegates which observers commented on was a fair and proper tribute to the narrow and ungenerous vision of those who were to lead the British Labour movement into the Second World War. As Aneurin Bevan said of the *Daily Herald*, soon after the war began, attacking the paper for the feebleness of its writing: 'It has the intellectual astringency of a parish magazine, and the scepticism of a Holy Roller.'[10]

The Labour movement, however, whatever the problems of these final years before the outbreak of war, was far from being unchanged by the tempestuous events of the previous twenty years. The majority of organized workers, and their trade union leaders, were still basically labourist in their social and political attitudes, but it was no longer the world of 1918. Socialist ideas had now become more widely disseminated than ever before. The writings of Tawney, Cole and Laski, with H. N. Brailsford as the interpreter in the world of socialist journalism, were debated and discussed in more sophisticated terms than in earlier periods of the modern movement, and the publications of the Left Book Club provided a socialist literature of great variety. It was not all, it may be agreed, of equal quality. There was, as yet, hardly a Marxist culture, but for the first time, outside the ranks of *Plebs* readers, members of the Labour colleges, and the small Communist Party of the 1920s, there was a serious discussion of Marx and Marxist ideas, and the availability of the classics of Marxism was being slowly improved. With the political developments already considered above, there was now the possibility of a more extended development of radical and socialist ideas, irrespective of the Labour leadership, if the general situation in Britain was encouraging; and that is just what the conditions of war were to provide.[11]

There is one further matter to be remarked upon. There have been two periods in the twentieth century when left groups have exercised a strong influence upon the ordinary members of the mainstream Labour movement. In the years before the First World War, a mixed group of organizations and individuals generated a general movement of ideas and militant practice which helped to extend the considerable industrial unrest. In the second period, from about 1935 to 1945, it was the Communist Party which was the organizer of ideas and practice with a marked impact upon the wider movement. These were years when there was a general coincidence of ideas and policies between the Communist Party and the left in both the unions and the Labour Party; and given the dedication and organizational abilities of the Communist Party, the consequences were wide ranging and, in some matters, long term in working themselves out. The reference is to the development of a Marxist intellectual tradition and the assumption, by industrial militants of the 1930s, of official positions in the trade union movement in the twenty years or so after the end of the Second World War. But the more momentous fact was the disruption of the links which bound the Communist Party to the left, and even the left-centre of the movement, after the coming to power of the Attlee Government in 1945. In a remarkably short space of time the policies of the Cold War had brought to an end the *de facto* united front between the Communist Party and the Labour left; and never again, in the forty years which followed, was any left group or groups to exercise any significant influence upon the mainstream of organized labour or its political organizations. Single-issue campaigns were still possible, as with the movement against the American war in Vietnam, but there was no sustained relationship, and this was especially true of the trade unions; and as will be considered below, this general failure of all the left groups, including the Communist Party, has had quite striking political consequences.

5
The Labour Governments: 1945–51

The end of the war in Europe in May 1945 was followed by a general election in which the Labour Party, contrary to most predictions, won an overwhelming victory – with 47.8 per cent of the total vote against the Tories' 39.8 per cent, and with 393 seats in a House of Commons of 640. And this in spite of a relatively low poll among voters in the armed forces whose majority support for Labour was generally recognized. The Labour victory was unexpected largely because of Winston Churchill's personal standing and popular esteem among the British people. What defeated him was that the electorate clearly distinguished the man from the Conservative Party he led. The memories of the pre-1939 Tory governments had taken on a new appreciation in the consciousness of ordinary people. Now what they remembered was unemployment and the means test, symbolized by the hunger marches which only a minority had supported when they occurred. There had developed a popular radicalism that emerged out of the ways in which the war had perforce to be conducted, and which contradicted the remembered experiences of the years before 1939. To describe, however, the six years of war as a people's war, without qualification, would be to miss the contradictions involved in the mobilization of a highly conservative society; but what cannot also be missed was the extension of democratic ideas and practices that did take place, and the enhanced expectations of the future that became a firmly embedded political fact. It was a fact mixed with much cynicism – what had happened after 1918 was a stubborn part of folk memory – but that the future might be different provided the Labour Party with a bedrock of support which steadily enlarged as the anti-Fascist character of the war became more plain. The heroism and sacrifice of the Russian people invoked a widespread respect and sympathy that over-rode the anti-Sovietism of the 1939–41 years, following the Nazi–Soviet Pact, and was itself a major influence in the moderate politicization of quite large numbers of the British people.

A revealing indication of the deepening anti-Fascist atti-tudes was the occasion of the release from prison of Oswald Mosley and his wife in November 1943. They had been interned with other members of Fascist organizations in the aftermath of the fall of France in the summer of 1940. The aristocratic connections of the Mosley and the Mitford families were continuously active in attempts first to improve their living conditions and then to secure their release – aided by libertarians such as the Labour MP Richard Stokes – and Herbert Morrison, the Home Secretary, came under growing pressure. Mosley had phlebitis, and the prison doctors finally recommended his release on the grounds that complications might set in, and Mosley might die in prison. Morrison announced his intention to release the Mosleys to the war cabinet on 17 November 1943 and three days later they were let out at an early hour of the morning, and put under house arrest. After the war, when he was finally free, Mosley enga-ged in political activity of varied kinds, all ineffectual, and managed to live until 1980, almost all the time in apparently good health.

The release of Mosley created an intense uproar in the country. 'Sackloads of letters of protest arrived at the Home Office,'[1] and the National Council of Labour quickly dissoci-ated itself from the action of the Government, as did the major unions. It was not mainly or wholly a Communist-organized protest nor was it a 'storm in a tea-cup', as Mosley's biographer inaccurately described what happened.[2] For Morrison it was the 'biggest storm' in his wartime career, and only the intruding events of a war that was now rapidly approaching its climax allowed the issue to die away in the New Year.

This episode was only one, if certainly one of the more spectacular, of the events that illuminated the political radicalization that was taking place. The success in by-elections of the wartime Common Wealth Party, the impressive increase in the membership and industrial strength of the trade union movement, the growth of the Communist Party and its considerable influence on the factory floor: these were all part of the shift towards the political left. Gallup polls had begun to be taken in Britain in the mid 1930s, and the trend in the polls showed a steady change in political attitudes from 1942 on. The Gallup prediction for the 1945 general election was remarkably accurate, even though very little notice was taken in these years of opinion forecasting. Among the armed forces the causes of a developing radicalism have been much debated. Some politicians later put a good deal of emphasis upon the Army Bureau of Current Affairs (ABCA) although its impact was, in practice, very patchy. Some debating forums, of which the Cairo Parliament was the best known, were important in helping to politicize sections of the army, but it would seem reasonable to argue that the general influences which affected the civilian population in Britain also contributed to changing attitudes among serving men and women; although the reaction against the incompetence, arbitrariness and class divisions of service life must certainly not be excluded from any analysis.

One important feature of wartime life in Britain was the increase in radio-listening and the growth in reading, both at least in part due to the wartime black-out and the difficulties of traditional social activities in leisure time. The radio was an important educator and the circulation of left-wing and anti-establishment literature was considerable. There was nothing on the Tory side to compare with *Guilty Men*, a vigorously written indictment of the politicians who had been active in the appeasement of Nazi Germany. It was published in July 1940, and sold nearly a quarter of a million copies in spite of a distribution ban by the main London wholesalers. Later titles, also published by Gollancz, included *The Trial of Mussolini* and *Your M.P.* The Labour Party manifesto of 1945, *Let us Face the Future*, insisted that it was 'a Socialist Party, and proud of it', and defined its ultimate purpose as 'the establishment of the Socialist Commonwealth of Great Britain – free, democratic, efficient, progressive, public spirited, its material resources organized in the service of the British people'. In sum, the manifesto provided a statement of the values which contrasted sharply with the practice of the prewar Tory governments, and it evoked a sympathetic resonance from within the greater part of the working people and a number of middle-class groups. Wartime controls had achieved a rough approximation to equality of sacrifice – less effective than was often appreciated – but the principles involved had come to be widely accepted, and the declarations of the Labour Party on domestic matters were listened to with understanding and sympathy. What the Labour Party, or rather the Labour leadership, meant by their rhetoric was the establishment of a comprehensive system of social security, broadly along the lines of the 1942 Beveridge Report that had so captivated the British people, together with specific measures of nationalization: the Bank of England, the basic energy industries, transport and iron and steel. It was only the last that was to arouse serious opposition. Full or nearly full employment was assumed. The programme was not a socialist one, although it was usually described as such, but it went as far as the traditional Labour socialists had always accepted would be practicable. If the whole programme of public ownership was completed, some 80 per cent of industry would remain in private hands, and there were no plans for altering in any fundamental way the highly uneven distribution of capital ownership. Nevertheless, the programme represented a marked advance on previous statements by Labour, and the proposals for social security, with the addition of children's allowances, completed the bitty, piecemeal legislation that had begun with the Liberal governments of pre-1914.

*

The first Labour Government, which lasted from the summer of 1945 to February 1950, has received a general approval from historians as well as from the Labour movement itself. The Attlee administration is now regarded by the Labour leadership today as an example of what Labour socialism can achieve, both in terms of policies and in execution; and the fortieth anniversary in 1985 was saluted with nostalgic celebrations. The second Attlee government, from February 1950 to October 1951, obtained nearly a million more votes than the Tories but had a majority of only five; and for many reasons it was a thing of shreds and tatters, culminating in a disastrous budget by Gaitskell, the Chancellor of the Exchequer.

What, then, did the Attlee Government achieve in the years after the end of the war? Certainly a Britain with a Tory majority in parliament would have had a quite different, and undoubtedly more turbulent, history, in spite of the apparent consensus that informed the leading members of the coalition Government of Churchill. The goodwill that Attlee and his colleagues enjoyed among the majority of ordinary people was immense, and it encouraged an ease of transition to a peacetime economy that would have been denied to a Conservative administration. The introduction of a comprehensive scheme of social benefits was seen as a major break with the past, although there were compromises within the National Health Service, and much of the finance for social services was an internal transfer of income within the working classes themselves; but these were not matters about which concern was expressed, even when they were known about. Children's allowances and a free and comprehensive health service meant significant advances for working people and not least for working-class women. The most important factor, however, in living standards was full employment. Demobilization was carried through as effectively as resources permitted, and wartime experience helped considerably in the redeployment of the millions from the armed forces. The 1945 Distribution of Industry Act – passed by the coalition Government – was vigorously used to establish industry in the former depressed areas; wartime controls were mostly continued; production increased steadily with imports kept down and exports greatly expanded. By 1950 manufacturing output was up by 34 per cent compared with 1937, while exports of manufactured goods had increased by 60 per cent between the two dates.

The leading members of the Attlee Government had considerable ministerial experience as a result of their years in the Churchill coalition. When they took office at the end of the war in Europe – which was quickly followed by the surrender of Japan – they were confronted with three outstanding problems. The first was the fulfilment of the hopes of the British people for a postwar world that was different from that of 1939: hopes that had been largely responsible for the Labour victory. Above all this meant full employment and the introduction of a range of social services on a universal basis. The second main question for the new ministers was the place of Britain in the world. Was Britain still a world power of the first class? There was still a British Empire, many parts of which were increasingly restive, with some, like the subcontinent of India, on the edge of open revolt; and in terms of material power a realistic appraisal of Britain's position would have developed many doubts. The largest share by far of war materials for the western allies had been produced by the United States, and the greater part of the destruction of the German army had been the responsibility of the Russians. The third problem followed ineluctably from the responses that were given to the first two questions. If Labour's domestic promises were to be honoured, they could be financed only from within, from external earnings or from a combination of both. The financial problems were inevitably worsened by the effects of six years of war: the considerable sale of overseas investments; the conversion of export industries to war production and the dramatic fall in export earnings; and finally, the fact that after the introduction of Lend-Lease the overseas commitments of the UK had been met increasingly by American dollars. The most favourable situation for Britain after the end of the war with Japan would have been a rapid switch to the exporting sectors; a drastic and speedy reduction in overseas financial commitments; and then a gentle phasing out, over several years, of American aid. The first of these requirements, as already noted, was achieved through an efficient demobilization, the use of controls to keep down imports, and the considerable pressure by Government for exports. It was a seller's market, and by 1950 some 25 per cent of world trade in manufactures was supplied by the United Kingdom.

The other two problems were conflated into one central strand of policy that carried heavy financial obligations. All the leading politicians, the civil servants in Whitehall and what constituted public opinion in the country at large, were convinced that Britain remained a great power and must continue to play the role of a great power. What this meant in practical politics in the world after 1945 was that Britain, the greatest imperialist nation, must remain the centre of its traditional Empire. There would be changes, of course, and some countries would achieve their independence, but for the rest the old order would continue. Indian independence was the most important single issue, and on this the Labour movement was united. India had long been at the centre of Labour's concerns with imperial questions – which were not very marked, it should be noted – and independence for India was accepted. On this matter Attlee was clear and determined; but apart from some other fairly minor exceptions – Ceylon, for example, where the British military presence was carefully safeguarded – Britain assumed its prewar role. The Labour leadership held broadly the same views on Empire as their Tory opponents. As Ernest Bevin told the House of Commons on 21 February 1946, six months after the end of the war with Japan:

> When I say I am not prepared to sacrifice the British Empire, what do I mean? I know that if the British Empire fell, the greatest collection of free nations would go into the limbo of the past, or it would be a disaster.

There was, however, a great deal more in the matter of overseas commitments than the demands of the British Empire, heavy in financial terms though these were. Indeed, the traditional assessment of the Labour Government of 1945 has been of an administration that began peacefully the processes of decolonization, although that, too, when the mountains of dead Hindus and Moslems in India are recalled, is not quite the simple story that is lodged firmly in the folk memory of the Labour movement. Britain had played a major part in the victory over Fascism and it was assumed by everyone in positions of power that Britain would also play a major part in the postwar settlement. But world politics are always matters of competing trends and conflicting interests. In Britain's case, there were questions of Empire and the strategic factors which followed therefrom; direct national interests in commerce and trade which often were in conflict with the United States; the anti-Communism and especially the anti-Sovietism that had been a central part of British foreign policy since the Revolution of 1917; and the defence and support of other imperialist powers who, in the aftermath of the war, were threatened by the rise of national liberation movements. The phrase was not used, but the domino effect of a successful anti-imperialist struggle was well understood.

Two examples will suffice and both, it should be noted, were under way well before the public manifestations of what became known as the Cold War. The antecedents of the Cold War go back to the October revolution of 1917, but we may begin with the spring of 1940 when Winston Churchill formed his coalition Government: the one great moment of his reactionary life – save for his few Liberal years before 1914 – when humanity must accord him respect and honour. Without Churchill the forces of prewar appeasement, still very powerful in the Conservative Party and the establishment generally, might have engineered a further version of Munich; it remains one of the interesting countervailing questions of twentieth-century history. During his years as Prime Minister Churchill hardly concerned himself with domestic affairs and he was involved almost wholly with world politics about which he had certain clear objectives. One was his conviction about Britain's role as an imperialist power; his opposition to the very moderate Tory reforms in India during the 1930s was only the best-known illustration of his views. A second was his deep-seated hatred of Communism and the Soviet Union. He had taken a leading part in the military intervention after 1918, and during the Second World War he became increasingly concerned at the political consequences in Europe of the growing successes of the Red Army against the German armies on the eastern front; and not least of the increasing importance of native Communists in the various national liberation movements. Churchill's intervention in Greece in the autumn and winter of 1944 was the first direct military intervention against any resistance movement and it took place six months before the war in Europe ended. Its purposes were to contain and if possible to eliminate the resistance movement, to restore the Greek monarchy backed by a right-wing government, and thereby to safeguard what was still considered to be a major strategic life-line to the oilfields of the Middle East and to India. The decision to intervene was not a sudden one, for the strategic importance of Greece had long been an established part of British military and political thinking. In August–September 1943 Konni Zilliacus wrote a private report for a Fabian study group on the future international situation as it was then developing. His central argument was that since 1917 the containment of the forces of social revolution had been one of the central threads of world politics, and he identified the areas in which major conflict could be expected in Europe once the war against Fascism was over. On Greece he emphasized Churchill's 'open partisanship on behalf of the Greek King, who has a black record of hostility to democracy, and of pro-fascism.'[3] The contrast with Churchill's attitude towards Yugoslavia is illuminating.[4]

We shall not know the influence of the Greek intervention upon the general policy of the Soviet Government until the Russian archives are open, but the vigorous support by the Labour leaders in the coalition Government ought to have warned Labour movement in Britain of what to expect in the future. When the intervention broke out into the fighting in Athens in early December 1944, there was widespread disquiet and opposition. At a one-day conference of the Labour Party on 18 December 1944, Ernest Bevin provided a total defence of Churchill's policy in Greece. It was answered in a short speech by Aneurin Bevan with the following comment:

> Mr Bevin has described what is happening in Greece. I have no time to answer him. But there is one complete answer. Only three bodies of public opinion in the world have gone on record in his support, namely Fascist Spain, Fascist Portugal and the majority of Tories in the House of Commons.

Bevan described Bevin's statement as 'garbled and inadequate where it was not unveracious'. When the Labour Government took over in the summer of 1945 there was no change in the policy towards Greece. No issue remained more controversial and for the first two years of Bevin's tenure as Foreign Secretary Greece was the main target of criticism in foreign affairs from within the British Labour movement. Then the Cold War began to envelop the opposition, and controversy diminished sharply. Aneurin Bevan was a member of the Labour cabinet throughout.

Greece was, however, only the first casualty of what many at the time of the 1945 general election thought would be a 'socialist' foreign policy. Even more revealing, perhaps, was the six months' 'police action' in Indo-China. Here there was no direct strategic issue for Britain but what perhaps may be described as old-fashioned imperialism; or, to be more accurate, one old-fashioned imperialist helping another. It is a story that has mostly been forgotten and one largely written out of British history books. The third volume of Alan Bullock's massive biography of Ernest Bevin, which deals only with the years of his foreign secretaryship, has a few incidental references to Indo-China, the most apposite being two sentences on page 32. Indonesia, where the British played an identical role to that in Indo-China, is given a good deal more space because of the extended fighting which went on for a much longer period.

In Indo-China the French colonial administration – strongly pro-Vichy during the war – was in serious danger of being eliminated at the end of the war by the indigenous liberation movement. The Vietminh took power in Hanoi in mid-August 1945 – a few days after the Japanese surrender – and at the end of the same month the Committee of the south, largely but not wholly led by Communists, took over Saigon. The Vietminh were much weaker in the South, and continued to accept the need for co-operation with the British and the Americans in the belief that their demand for independence from the hated French would be accepted. In Paris, de Gaulle was inflexible concerning the inviolability of the French Empire, and its restoration, but they had no military power in the Far East to impose their wishes. So the British moved in, using mostly Indian and Gurkha troops. The British General in command, Douglas D. Gracey, was very clear in his own mind that Indo-China was to remain French; and so was the Foreign Office in London. The operation began in mid-September 1945. Within a week of arriving Gracey had declared what in effect was martial law; newly released French prisoners were armed, the main buildings in Saigon were taken over and military control was steadily tightened. Since there were not enough troops to ensure 'order', Japanese troops were employed; and very satisfactory they proved. An American journalist, Harold Isaac, reported that 'the British were delighted with the discipline shown by their late enemy and were often warmly admiring, in the best playing field tradition, of their fine military qualities. It was all very comradely.'[5] By the end of 1945 all that was now needed was for the French to move into Indo-China in sufficient force; and this they did by the end of January 1946, and the British moved out. It was a most exemplary operation. In the British House of Commons on 28 January 1946, Noel Baker gave the figures of the casualties since the first September landings: of 126 Allied dead three were British and thirty-seven Indian; but there was no precise information about the 'Annamites and Tonkinites who opposed our troops: it has been estimated that about 2,700 have been killed'. This was after all quite a modest beginning to the horrendous decades of bloodshed that were to follow, and Bullock was no doubt formally correct in writing that 'the British handed over with relief to the French in the spring of 1946'.

The continued commitment to policies similar to those in Greece and Indo-China throughout the world for the remainder of the life of the Labour Governments meant that there was no possibility of Britain becoming solvent financially without outside help; and that could only mean American dollars. When Truman abruptly cancelled Lend-Lease within a fortnight of the ending of the war with Japan – something the British had never anticipated – Keynes had to be sent to Washington to negotiate the largest possible draught of dollars on what was assumed to be the continuation of Anglo-American wartime collaboration: one of a growing number of miscalculations in London concerning the dynamics of American policy. There had already been serious conflicts over nuclear energy and the atom bomb and these were to continue, but because of the secrecy which enveloped nuclear development they were known only to a handful of politicians and civil servants in Whitehall. Until the Labour Government took office, no Labour member of Churchill's war cabinet knew anything about nuclear matters; and Attlee continued the secrecy by excluding his full cabinet from knowledge of these questions. When Attlee decided to manufacture a British bomb – the decision was taken in early 1947 – it was not the cabinet which was consulted but an *ad hoc* committee, picked by Attlee, which included Sir John Anderson because he had been much involved during the Churchill period. Anderson was known to be bitterly anti-Labour. And further, in order to remove the decision about a British bomb from vulgar discussion, Attlee instructed the Treasury to 'hide' the £100 million that was needed for initial development in the Government financial estimates. Churchill discovered this when he returned to office late in 1951.[6]

To return to September 1945, when Keynes went to Washington to negotiate what he confidently informed ministers would be a free gift or grant in aid. There would be no question, Keynes explained, of a loan which would have to be repaid, and most people who were involved in the discussions seemed to have believed him. But Keynes was hopelessly wrong, for he failed to appreciate the changes

[93]

which had taken place in Washington after the death of
Roosevelt. Moreover what experience had not apparently
taught Keynes was that relations between capitalist states
were not based upon personal relationships or liberal-minded
rationality, but upon self-interest as conceived by the particular national interest group or groups who happen to
control or influence national policies. Throughout the war
years there had been very sharp differences between various
parts of the American administration in their attitudes
towards Britain – the conflicts between the Treasury and the
State Department are only the best known; and the tricky
way that Land-Lease funds were carefully calculated to
ensure that Britain would not be able to build up too large a
reserve should have alerted London to the sophistication of
the Americans in world affairs, and their ability to learn very
quickly what the options on their own self-interest were. It
was one of the many illusions the British had about the
Americans that in the immediate aftermath of the war there
was a real possibility of the United States repeating the
withdrawal into isolationism that characterized the years
after the end of the First World War: an error which confused
temporary trends in some parts of American public opinion
with the tough appreciation of America's role in the world
that permeated most of the leading groups of policy-makers
in Washington. The negotiations for the American loan are
usually discussed in the terms expounded by Hugh Dalton in
his memoirs:

> So, as the talks went on, we retreated, slowly and with a
> bad grace and with increasing irritation, from a free gift to
> an interest-free loan, and from this again to a loan bearing
> interest; from a larger to a smaller total of aid; and from the
> prospect of loose strings, some of which would be only
> general declarations of intention, to the most unwilling
> acceptance of strings so tight that they might strangle our
> trade and, indeed, our whole economic life.[7]

What Dalton does not discuss, nor is it usually mentioned in
this context, is that the Americans were conducting parallel
discussions on the issue of American control or repossession

of a large number of bases round the world. In a letter dated 7 November 1945 Byrnes, the Secretary of State, sent Bevin a list of such bases. Some the Americans wished to continue in joint control with the British. The Embassy in Washington made it clear that a healthy co-operation from the Foreign Office in London would encourage the prospects of a deal over the loan; and when these facts are put alongside the policies that were developing within the Pentagon, the suggestion that the Americans needed the sophisticated British to help guide them through the complexities of the world after war, must be characterized as naïve and a matter of serious misjudgement. It is not widely known that already in October 1945 the theory of the 'first strike', in the new age of the atomic bomb, was being seriously considered within the top military groups in America; or that soon after the US Strategic Air Command was established in the early summer of 1946, Spaatz himself visited England to obtain an agreement whereby British bases could be used by the Americans in an emergency for atom bomb missions. The negotiations were conducted by Air Chief Marshall Lord Tedder and five RAF bases were allocated to be made ready for the B-29 bombers. None of this was made public, and even when, at the time of the Berlin blockade in July 1948, American airforce groups began to be permanently stationed in Britain, they were first described in the House of Commons as 'visits of goodwill and for training purposes'.[8]

To return to the American Loan agreement of December 1945 which had still to be ratified by Congress. The justification for the loan and its onerous conditions was vigorously defended by Dalton in the Commons and by Keynes in the House of Lords. But Keynes himself began to appreciate the true nature of the problem. In a revealing memorandum written on 22 February 1946, a few months before his death, he noted that 'it comes out in the wash that the American Loan is primarily required to meet the political and military expenditure overseas';[9] and he went on to say that without these commitments Britain could 'scrape through' without any serious interruption to the domestic programme the Labour Government was undertaking. The Labour Government, however, did not cut back its financial responsibilities overseas, and although there was some opposition in the cabinet – from Dalton especially – there was no serious threat to the foreign policy objectives set by Bevin and the Foreign Office.

It is necessary to ask how it came about that the Labour Government, with the most radical mandate any reforming government had been given within the period of the modern Labour movement, came to accept from its earliest days the continuation of the old imperialist order and then the policies of the Cold War in which, in a number of respects, it had indeed been the front runner. We must begin with the two dominating personalities of the 1945 Government; Attlee and Bevin. The relationships between personality and social structure, within a network of interest groups and entrenched positions, are always complex, intricate and often unpredictable, and especially one would assume a tension and strain in the case of radicals. But there was nothing of stress between Attlee and Bevin and the established order which they now controlled. The political conflict within the Parliamentary Labour Party in the whole period of Labour Government was between the leadership and a left wing on the back benches; and the striking thing about the Attlee administration was that this conflict actually decreased in its later years. It is true that a few judicious expulsions from the Party assisted the processes of accommodation but that is not the main story.

Attlee was a much tougher personality than his physical appearance, or his manner of speaking, often suggested. He was an excellent chairman of committees, an efficient co-ordinator of the policies he wished to achieve, and ruthless in his dealings with colleagues whose services he no longer required. In the 1930s he exhibited a sympathy with the radical causes of that decade – he went to Spain, for example, and actually spoke on a hunger march platform in 1936 – but his years in the war cabinet had exorcized these unnatural tendencies in a Labour leader, and by 1945 he was as committed an anti-Communist and as hostile to the Soviet Union as senior civil servants had come to expect of their political masters. Attlee, however, was more perceptive than many in certain areas of foreign policy and he showed a realism, set down in memoranda of 1946 and 1947, that was alien to both the Chiefs of Staff and the Foreign Office. But nothing came of his initiatives, which would have drastically reduced Britain's commitments in the Middle East, and the reason was Bevin. Within the top leadership of the Labour Government Attlee was dependent upon Bevin's support. The attempts that were made to replace Attlee could never succeed without Bevin's support, and this was never given. In return Bevin had his way in foreign affairs, although it must be emphasized that in the matter of the central thrust of British policy against the Soviet Union there were no differences between the two men. [10]

The majority of the senior members of the Foreign Office at the time Bevin took the position of Secretary of State were intelligent, sophisticated reactionaries whose traditional hostility to the Soviet Union went back to the 1917 revolution. They were for the most part convinced of their superiority over their contemporaries in other chancelleries and not least in respect of the Americans. Like most other conservatives they were troubled by the Labour victory of 1945, and no doubt were immensely relieved when Bevin was substituted for Dalton in the last-minute changes that Attlee made to his senior appointments. Sir Alexander Cadogan, permanent Under-secretary of the Foreign Office, wrote with pleasant frankness in his personal diary of his assessment of the new situation he and his colleagues were confronted with. The occasion was the resumed Potsdam conference of July 1945:

> I think we may do better with Bevin than with any of the other Labourites. I think he's broadminded and sensible, honest and courageous. But whether he's an inspired Foreign Minister or not I don't know. He's the heavyweight of the Cabinet and will get his own way with them, so if he can be put on the right line, that might be all right. [11]

The right line was, of course, the continuation of the existing line that had developed during the Churchill–Eden years. But Bevin did not have to be converted to the traditional attitudes of the Foreign Office, for their general thinking was already part of his own emotional and political reactions. Bevin had two major deficiencies that were of inestimable value to his Foreign Office advisers. The first was his lack of practical experience of foreign affairs and international relations. He had been a member of the war cabinet, and was therefore aware of the general direction of events, and according to a later statement by Eden there were no occasions when Bevin expressed basic disagreement with the policies that the coalition Government were pursuing. It is, of course, one thing to sit in cabinet when foreign affairs are being discussed, and a quite different matter when these are your departmental concerns. It remains true that Bevin was not at all equipped intellectually for the position of Foreign Secretary except in so far as his prejudices, always strongly and powerfully expressed, fitted very easily into the general approach of his senior officials. There was a second, related deficiency which the Foreign Office must have immediately discovered; that in Bevin's mind there was a vacuum about what a Labour, let alone a socialist, foreign policy involved. It was not going to be too difficult to put Bevin on the 'right line'.

There were certain major premises which Bevin and the Foreign Office shared. One was the anti-Communism and anti-Sovietism already discussed which in practical terms meant an outright opposition to national liberation movements everywhere and an unswerving opposition to the Soviet Union. Second, there was a fervent commitment to the 'great power' thesis. Again and again, from the leading politicians on both sides of the House of Commons, from the Chiefs of Staff and their advisers, and from within Whitehall, there was a steady, unwavering understanding that Britain remained a first-class power alongside the United States and the Soviet Union. The illusion was powerful and pervasive, and while it was misguided and untrue, it is understandable in terms of the contribution that Britain had made to the war against Fascism. To those who had come through the war it was inconceivable that Britain should not continue as a leading power in the counsels of the postwar world. What is interesting is that not one person of any political standing within the United Kingdom was prepared to state publicly that the war had changed fundamentally the balance of forces within world politics, and that henceforth Britain could only expect to play the part of a major second-class power. The Americans were never in doubt, and by 1945 they were quite clear that while Britain was still important in world affairs, and certainly important to the Americans in terms of their imperial interests and their political expertise, the role of Britain could only be subordinate to themselves. The so-called 'special relationship' was an invention of the British to which the Americans never subscribed except when it suited their national self-interest. The history of the Anglo-American relations in the matter of nuclear energy and the atom bomb is only one of a number of illuminating examples of the ruthlessness with which the Americans conducted their dealings with the British. But the illusions lived on in London, and Bevin himself probably believed in the myth of the 'naïve' Americans to the end of his life.

The crucial question for the historian is why the opposition to Bevin's foreign policy within the Labour movement in Britain proved so lacking in stamina and commitment, and why, if one takes the decades which followed, did there continue to exist the remarkable agreement on all fundamentals concerning foreign affairs between the mainstream Labour movement and the Conservative establishment. It was not the absence of criticism during the first two years of Bevin's term of office. Intervention in Greece remained the most important single issue of these first two years, with a considerable movement in the country at large against the continuation of the Churchill policy. In June 1946 the Labour Party conference at Bournemouth – the first since the election victory of 1945 – showed that the one exception to enthusiastic support of the Attlee administration was foreign affairs. On a wide range of issues, including recruitment to the Foreign Office staff, there was vigorous criticism of Labour's policies, summed up in Konni Zilliacus' bitter comment that Bevin was making himself 'the white hope of a Black International'. Bevin won the debate, and won it decisively, but the criticisms remained. In the following

November an amendment to the address was tabled by fifty-three Labour MPs expressing the 'urgent hope' that the Government would 'renew and recast its conduct of foreign affairs', and thereby provide 'a democratic and constructive socialist alternative to an otherwise inevitable conflict between American capitalism and Soviet Communism'. R. H. S. Crossman moved the amendment in the House of Commons on 17 November 1946 and since Bevin was in New York, Attlee replied to the debate. The matter was not pressed to a vote but it represented the most serious critique of Bevin's foreign policy ever to come from within the Parliamentary Labour Party.

A few months later, in May 1947, the *New Statesman* published 'Keep Left', a pamphlet drafted by Crossman, Michael Foot and Ian Mikardo, and signed by twelve other back-bench MPs. In its summing up the pamphlet listed 'Twenty things to do now'. They included a more rapid demobilization of the armed forces; a refusal to accept the division of the world into hostile blocs, and a repudiation of the Truman proposals for 'collective security against Communism'; the ending of staff talks with the United States; renunciation of atomic weapons; withdrawal of British forces in Greece, Palestine and Egypt; and integration of Germany into a planned European economy. Very soon after, the Labour Party published *Cards on the Table*, written by Denis Healey, a persuasive and influential defence of the foreign policy of the Attlee Government. At the Margate conference of the Labour Party, at the end of May 1947, the critics were still powerful but their impact upon the delegates was declining; and from this time on the opposition towards Bevin's conduct of foreign affairs began to weaken in a quite remarkable way.

The *Keep Left* group were never tightly organized and Crossman, a man of distinctly flexible principles, proved easily influenced by changing events which he was to interpret in ways favourable to Bevin's approach. One was the Marshall Plan, first put forward in a formal way by Secretary of State George Marshall at a speech at Harvard on 5 June 1947. It was a speech that had been well prepared, and no one who has read the massive documentation that is available from American sources will believe the fairy story, invented by the British and sustained to our own day by British historians, that it was Bevin's imagination that picked up the key phrases in Marshall's speech and turned them into a major diplomatic initiative. As Dean Acheson wrote of the discussions in the weeks *before* Marshall's speech, when the matters of European aid were being considered at the top levels of the American administration: 'Surely the plan should be a European Plan and come – or at any rate appear to come – from Europe. *But the United States must run the show.* And it must start running it now.[12] The italics were Acheson's. The central question to be answered is the extent to which the Marshall Plan gave the United States political leverage within western Europe. Milward's strongly revisionist thesis is that Marshall Aid did not save Western Europe from collapse because Western Europe was not collapsing, but it did allow some governments to continue the policies domestically and abroad which had brought about the 1947 payment's crisis.[13]

Britain did well out of Marshall Aid in that about 25 per cent of all Marshall Aid-financed imports went to the United Kingdom; but there were political consequences which have continued to our own day. The way was eased for the permanent establishment of American air forces in the United Kingdom, and it was understood that Britain would increase its defence expenditure. On the matter of the formal establishment of American bases in Britain, it was the Berlin blockade that provided the official reasons for agreement, although the American military leaders had always wanted European bases and Britain had always been understood to be the obvious location. By mid-1950 all the airfields agreed in the Spaatz–Tedder discussions of 1946 had become B-29 bases, with the exception of Bassingbourn, near Cambridge. Burtonwood, near Warrington in Lancashire, was becoming the major supply centre for the increasing number of American planes. In the same year 1950, *before* the Korean War began, four new airfields were given to the USAF for full development. These were Greenham Common, Upper Heyford, Fairford and Brize Norton. And so the story has continued. By 1984 there were 135 American military bases in Britain, most of them operational, some still being planned or rebuilt. Within this total there are at least five known US nuclear weapons stores: the unsinkable aircraft carrier, the ultimate control of which rests with the President of the United States. Ultimate control, in this context, refers to the decision to use nuclear weapons.[14]

The widespread acceptance of what has become the client status of Britain, in military terms, goes back to the period when the 'Keep Left' group underwent its rapid disintegration, or perhaps change of mind and heart would be more accurate. There was a foreign policy debate in the House of Commons early in 1948, and Crossman, who had been so active in the opposition to Bevin, explained in what he himself described as frank terms where he now stood: 'My own views about America,' he said 'have changed a great deal in the last six months. Many members have had a similar experience. I could not have believed six months ago that a plan of this sort would have been worked out in detail with as few political conditions'. The pro-Americanism of Crossman and most of his colleagues in the 'Keep Left' group were further strengthened by their political appreciation of Truman and his 'fair deal' election campaign, and Truman's victory was warmly welcomed by most of the Labour backbenchers.

There were other factors which also contributed to the collapse of any principled opposition to Labour's foreign policy, and to the support of their vigorous anti-Communism. The most important was undoubtedly the rapid decline of sympathy with the Soviet Union and its postwar attitudes and policies. An enormous goodwill had built up during the later war years and it was, indeed, an essential part of the radicalization that was taking place among sections of the British people. But within a year to eighteen months this sympathy and support had changed into its opposite. It is now accepted by most orthodox historians that the Soviet Union was not an aggressive power in the years after the war; that she was very properly concerned with the security problems on her western frontiers, but that with her immense losses in people and material it would have been impossible for Russia to engage once again in a major war. However, the facts of the Stalinist terror of the 1930s were becoming increasingly known in Western Europe, and it was not at all difficult to transpose the monstrous evils of Stalinism to external affairs. The Soviet Union – certainly under great provocation from the West – exhibited some monumental stupidities, and cruelties, in matters of foreign policies, of which the Communist takeover in Czechoslovakia and the break with Yugoslavia were among the most influential in their impact upon world opinion. The culminating point was the outbreak of the Korean War which aroused more hysteria among the anti-Soviet bloc than any other single issue, even though in this case the designated aggressor was Red China not the Soviet Union. It is only during the past decade or so that the Korean War has begun to be analysed in its real meaning in terms of a very complicated tangle of civil war and American intervention, but at the time it exercised a major influence upon the hardening of attitudes in the Cold War.

This was the background to the disintegration of an opposition to Bevin's foreign policies. There were a few independent socialists among the Parliamentary Labour Party who were not swept into the anti-Communist and anti-Soviet stream which was now moving so swiftly, but they were sharply curbed by the leadership and four Labour MPs were expelled from the Party: the most important being Konni Zilliacus, a former League of Nations civil servant with a remarkable understanding of the realities of world politics. At the same time as this revision of the situation on foreign affairs was taking place, a new appreciation of the achievements of the Labour administration was beginning, and it is to this we must now turn.

The introduction of a social welfare system meant that by 1950 Britain was spending about twice as much on each person compared with the year 1938; but the finance of welfare was largely a matter of a transfer of income from within the lower-income groups themselves. The direct and indirect taxes paid on average by families with less than £500 per year more than exceeded the current social expenditure, including the subsidies on food, the largest single item. More than half of the total raised in taxation came from the indirect taxation on drink and tobacco. The financial principles were based upon those of the social legislation of 1911, introduced by the Liberal Government of that year. But these were not the considerations that moved the many conservative groups in British society. At the centre of much of the political discussions of the postwar years was the steadily increasing conviction that egalitarianism was being pushed forward remorselessly at the expense of the middle ranks of society. It was a theme that the daily and weekly press constantly fed to its readers, and the argument, in political and academic circles, began to concentrate upon the redistribution of income. It was not a matter which had excited much interest before 1939 when national income studies were at their very beginning; and in the years after the war they were still in a very crude state: a fact which did not prevent large-scale deductions being made from the data available. From the early days of the Labour Government *The Economist*, normally believed to be a responsible journal, had been campaigning with some vigour on behalf of the downtrodden middle classes. Its editorial staff clearly believed the middle strata of society to be badly bleeding, and their efforts on behalf of middle-class health were both continuous and prodigious. This was especially so from about the middle of 1947 when *The Economist* swung decisively against the Labour Government. On 15 November 1947 it published a number of statistical tables which set out the material then available on the movement of wages, salaries and profits; and it went on to warn against any hard and fast deductions that might be made from a preliminary view of these statistics. *The Economist* concluded that little if any weight of interpretation should be put upon these data, although it invited its readers to make their own 'illuminating comparisons'. When *The Economist* returned to the theme of the downtrodden middle classes the qualifications of the article of 15 November were entirely forgotten. Now, on 3 January 1948, the journal published a major article on postwar income redistribution in which the conclusions arrived at were put forward as incontrovertible facts without any of the qualifications so carefully set out in the previous article of 15 November. The language used was often hysterical, and it will be appreciated that the popular press in these years went a long way beyond *The Economist* in exaggeration and hyperbole:

> it is as well to recall what has happened in recent years to the distribution of incomes in this country. The statistical evidence we examined in an article in *The Economist* of 15 November [1947]. The conclusion then reached was that, after making full allowance for changes in prices and in taxation, the real net income of the average wage-earner is between 10 and 35 per cent higher than in 1938 . . . At least 10 per cent of the national consuming power has been forcefully transferred from the middle classes and the rich to the wage-earners.

The literature on income redistribution swelled during the next decade. The Board of Inland Revenue's 92nd Report for 1948–9 surveyed the changes in the previous ten years, and concluded that there had been 'a very considerable redistribution of incomes' in favour of the wage-earning groups. The extraordinary unanimity of academic and political opinion was summed up by Professor Lionel Robbins. In an article in *Lloyds Bank Review*, he wrote that 'there is nothing particularly neutral in the operation of the present tax structure. Relentlessly year by year it is pushing us towards collectivism and propertyless uniformity.'

It was, of course, nonsense. Richart Titmus began the demolition of these irresponsible analyses in his 1962 *Income Distribution and Social Change*, and A. D. Atkinson and others in the last two decades have continued to provide academically respectable surveys of a very complicated statistical set of problems, but which certainly do not sustain the exaggerated arguments that have been briefly set out above. But more important than the exposé of the shoddiness and inaccuracy of the economic writing on income and wealth distribution in Britain in the postwar years was the fact that

[105]

the intellectuals who were influential within the counsels of the Labour Party and Labour Government themselves believed in the social revolution which had supposedly taken place, of which a radical income redistribution was but one component. What C. A. R. Crosland called 'The Transition from "Capitalism"' was the theme of a series of articles published in *New Fabian Essays*, which appeared in 1952. Few of the authors were quite as extreme as Crosland in their view of the supposed social revolution which was in process of occurring, but all worked from the assumption that major changes had taken place. Crosland, in his 1952 essay, defined capitalism as an industrialized society in which the greater part of economic activity is undertaken by privately-owned units, acting without interference by the state; and his definition of a post-capitalist society included what Burnham had originally called the 'managerial revolution', as a result of which the managers, not the owners, of property, controlled capitalist enterprise. It also involved the increasing intervention of the state, now 'an independent intermediate power'; and the wide-ranging forms of state intervention compared with the previous situation of *laissez-faire*, with the state acting as night watchman by itself, justified 'the statement that the capitalist era has now passed into history'.

These statements were repeated, although not quite in the stark illiteracy of *New Fabian Essays*, in Crosland's major contribution to socialist theory, *The Future of Socialism*, published in 1956. It was a volume which immediately became the benchmark for the socialist intellectuals of the Labour Party and which has continued to exercise its influence to our own day. The deputy-leader of the Labour Party published in 1986 a volume which was explicitly developing the arguments and themes of Crosland's book of thirty years earlier. Crosland accepted the considerable income redistribution that had supposedly taken place, and in his abridged and revised version of *The Future of Socialism* in 1964 he could still write that 'the distribution of personal income has become significantly more equal; and the change has been almost entirely at the expense of property incomes'. And he ended Part One, 'The Transformation of Capitalism', with words which clearly established his intellectual position:

> the proper definition of the word capitalism is a society with the essential social, economic, and ideological characteristics of Great Britain from the 1830s to the 1930s; and this, assuredly, the Britain of 1956 is not. And so, to the question 'Is this still Capitalism?', I would answer 'No'.

Crosland studied economics at the University of Oxford, at which institution the place of economic history in social studies has always been marginal. No one who knew anything of the history of the development of capitalism in Germany, or Japan, could possibly have assumed that capitalism as a system of economic organization may be defined as the absence of state intervention; but there is no point in pursuing the errors and omissions of historical analysis that spatter Crosland's work. Long before he died in 1977 the main arguments of *The Future of Socialism* had been falsified. Indeed, during the 1950s, when Crosland was writing his book, the capitalist class was enjoying a bonanza, the like of which had not before been experienced at any time during the twentieth century. From 1951, wrote Nicholas Davenport, 'the average rich man more than doubled his capital in the thirteen years to April 1964, without having to exercise his brains. If however he had invested his capital shrewdly he would have trebled it.' And this was only the beginning of the story. Already in the early 1950s the Inland Revenue Staff Federation ended their submission to the Royal Commission on Taxation by noting that 'the avoidance of tax, whether legal or illegal, is reaching the proportions of a social evil'; and the catalogue of the ways in which the rich have become richer would include an ever-lengthening list of new types of additional non-taxable income available to the directors and higher-paid executives of private enterprise, usually described by the euphemism 'fringe' benefits.

Crosland did not have to consider the dynamics of capitalist society since he took full employment and economic growth as given. The wrongheadedness of the Labour intellectuals after 1950 and the damage they inflicted upon the Labour movement by their disastrously incorrect analysis of postwar capitalism has lasted unto our own day. For those who looked about them with open eyes in the Britain of the 1950s the evidence of a massive shift in income distribution was not exactly overpowering. The differences in the way of life between the middle-class suburbs and the working-class areas of urban Britain were as obvious as they had been before 1939. By the end of the first decade after the war, however serious the financial or social haemorrhage the middle classes were suffering from, the fact of bleeding was not immediately apparent. The experience of daily life did not square with all the talk of massive social changes, and the inflated claims made by Labour publicists only increased a general disbelief. Full employment continued throughout the 1950s, and it was this above all that continued to encourage the hopelessly wrong conclusions which the Labour revisionists deduced from postwar economic and social trends.

The long-established belief that the Labour government of 1945 was a radical administration stemmed first and foremost, as already noted, from the welfare policies introduced before 1950, with the National Health Service undoubtedly the most important and the most influential. There is no question that a Conservative government would have established a less radical version of health care than that developed by Aneurin Bevan, although the latter's scheme was still a political compromise, especially with regard to the position of consultants within the NHS, and the continued existence of a private sector. Moreover, a number of its important projects – health centres being the best known – have largely remained unfulfilled. But for the rest a Conservative administration would probably have introduced a more or less comprehensive national insurance and benefits scheme, based upon the Beveridge report of 1942. Nevertheless, the implementation of the Labour Party's social welfare scheme within three years of taking office made a deep and lasting impression upon public opinion, and they confirmed the now general acceptance of collectivist support for the wide range of social casualties in modern industrial society. The problem for the Labour movement, which it has never solved down to the present, is not only that the basic structure of society has remained unchanged, but that capitalism, as a dynamically evolving system, constantly breeds new types of inequality and new categories of the poor; and all state welfare schemes ought regularly to be adjusted to take account of such changes.

The second main area of Labour's legislative programme was the nationalization of important industrial and service groups within the British economy. Social ownership of the means of production had always been accepted, from the early days of socialism, as a determining factor in the establishment of a socialist society; and the principle was endorsed in the famous clause four of the 1918 Labour Party Constitution. Unlike the issues of social welfare, however, there had been almost no discussion prior to 1945 of the place of nationalization within an industrial economy, or of the nature and character of the nationalization to be carried through. The only model the Labour Party had for taking any industry into state ownership was Herbert Morrison's ideas of the public corporation, based upon his own plan for the London Passenger Transport Board in the second minority Labour Government of 1929; and although there was some discussion of the issue of workers' control in the early 1930s – which Morrison rejected – there was no serious consideration in the years which followed; nor during the years of war. The first nationalization of the Labour Government was the Bank of England Act, a measure which illustrates the weaknesses of the leading politicians and their intellectual advisers. The left of the movement after the crisis of 1931 had argued for the nationalization of the whole banking system, not least because the belief that 1931 was at least in part a 'bankers' ramp' was common at the time. But Ernest Bevin and most of the trade union leaders were lukewarm; there was fear of an electoral backlash by the right wing of the Party; and Hugh Dalton with the group of young Labour intellectuals around Gaitskell and Evan Durbin provided strong economic arguments which suggested that so long as the central Bank was under complete government control the financial direction of the economy would be assured. The commercial banks and insurance companies were therefore left in the private sector, to exercise growing influence and power once wartime controls were removed. Moreover, there was no attempt made to introduce new thinking at the top administrative levels of the Bank of England: the Governor and Deputy Governor remained unchanged and the Court, or part-time executive board, was virtually the same although its numbers were reduced and its membership now included one right-wing trade unionist. Full compensation was paid, on dividends which had always been 12 per cent per annum on the Bank's capital. As *The Economist* wrote of the Bill when first published: 'It would take a very nervous heart to register a flutter at what is contained in the Bill. Nothing could be more moderate.'

The continued employment of existing experts and administrators and generous terms of compensation were to be accepted in all subsequent measures of nationalization. The second area of nationalization was the coal industry, and here further serious mistakes were made. Coal was an industry that was backward in the technical sense, with poor management, a serious lack of skilled mining engineers, a grossly inefficient national structure and the worst industrial relations of any industry sector in Britain. Taking the industry into state ownership was essential if the mining industry was to make its proper contribution to economic recovery and growth. The problems were clearly identified. In 1945 there was published what became known as the Reid Report, an official enquiry into the coal industry that was chaired by Charles Reid, the director of production at the Ministry of Fuel and Power. The report, which echoed previous enquiries, was a devastating indictment of the mining industry in private hands, although that was not its stated objective; and it was abundantly plain that the future of the industry would require a massive capital investment within a national plan, and radically different approaches in order to counter the deeply embedded hostility of the miners to management if industrial relations in the future were to be different from the past. There was no easy path forward, but what was needed above all else after the Government decision to nationalize was a realistic acceptance on the part of the miners that the old system had gone, and would not return. What the miners in fact got was an industry organized on a national basis, with a board, the chairman of which was the former managing director of a major mining combine – who was himself in favour of nationalization – and nine members which now included two senior trade unionists, both of whom resigned from their union positions. At all levels of industry below the national board there was no attempt to introduce any serious measure of worker's control, or worker participation, and this was to be true of later measures of nationalization.

The general result was that in industries like coal and the railways the levels of investment remained too low for the radical improvement in productivity that was required, and labour relations were more or less unaltered. Before the end of the first Labour Government in 1950 nationalization was already becoming a synonym for inefficiency and incompetence. Nationalizing broken-down industrial structures was not the best advertisement for social ownership, and political education of an imaginative kind was required if those within the particular industries, and society outside, were to comprehend the difficult problems involved. Political education did not come from the Labour Government, in the years after 1945, nor from the leaders of the trade union movement, nor from the mainstream of Labour intellectuals. Nationalization was still assumed by most Labour supporters to be the equivalent of a socialist measure, not needing justification, and the result was a growing disillusionment among ordinary people with the whole business of social ownership, and a general debasement of the idea of socialism itself.

State-owned industries, by their nature, do not have to be or to remain inefficient as some European experience has clearly demonstrated. But in Britain no section of the Labour movement for twenty years or so after 1945 seriously examined the structures of nationalized industries or offered new ways forward. Change in Britain has traditionally come about by instalments and piecemeal methods: partly because the vested interests have always been so powerful; partly also because reformers in Britain have always had great difficulty in escaping from contemporary modes of thought and what passes for orthodoxy. Middle-class reformist ideas have continued to exercise a powerful influence upon the Labour movement up to our own time. The dominant Fabian tradition is a mixture of anti-capitalist concepts and traditional ideas. We have already noted the Fabian illusion that state power is to be equated with a parliamentary majority at Westminster; and the leading ideas of bourgeois society have continued in the twentieth century, as in the decades after 1850, to determine an important part of the political and social theory of the Labour movement. The vaunted empiricism of the movement, while representing some strengths, has rested upon an intellectual foundation whose basic components have been supplied by liberal–conservative thinkers. Of all this there are many examples; Philip Snowden's absurd and tragic economic liberalism of the 1920s; the acceptance of the theory and practice of the eleven-plus technique of school selection; and the undeviating support for the assumptions and policies of the Cold War among the Labour leadership for the past forty years.

What needs to be emphasized for the years immediately after 1945 is that the welfare policies and highly conservative nationalization measures were slotted into a society that had remained unchanged in its fundamentals during the war; and which was not to witness any alteration in its basic postulates in the decades which followed. Indeed, it is one of the remarkable characteristics of Britain during the twentieth century that in spite of two world wars and a major economic crisis, the propertied groups, and their political representatives, have retained their economic and political power unimpaired. There have been changes in the relative balance of power between the different factions of property owners, but as a solid block of conservatism, including an important component of undiluted and exceedingly unpleasant reaction, they have not just survived but flourished. And so have their traditional institutions through which power and influence is organized and diffused throughout society. Class has remained the major factor in the recruitment to the key sectors of the state apparatus; the Armed Forces, the Judiciary, and the Civil Service. It is the latter of course – the administrative civil servants – who exercise the most direct influence upon decision making by the politicians of the government in power. Governments have to submit themselves to a popular vote every so many years, but the civil servants will continue until their normal retirement age of sixty. The Fulton committee, which reported in 1968, found that in the 1960s the administrative civil servants came overwhelmingly from the professional and managerial classes, and that of those who reported their university background some 70 per cent had been educated at Oxford or Cambridge, and about the same proportion had studied the humanities. Natural and scientific subjects were the educational background of only 13 per cent of all entrants. The salaries of top civil servants, as with those of the senior officers of the armed forces, and the senior judges, allow them a life style that continues to remove them from any contact, except in the course of their official duties, with the great majority of their fellow citizens. So it has always been; and so, after six years of war and another six years of the Labour Governments, it was to remain.

Education is always a useful index to the general state of the democratic process in an industrial society. The demand for a widening of educational opportunity had always been a vociferous, if minority trend, within the modern British Labour movement; but given the philistinism of the English towards education – attitudes inherited from the nineteenth century – progress had been slow. The interesting aspect for the historian of the debates within the Labour movement is the extent to which the existing class divisions came to be tolerated. Egalitarianism was inimical to the liberal tradition, and labourism, as the advanced form of nineteenth-century liberalism, took over many elements of its social thinking. When education came to be seriously considered in the debates on the postwar world during the years of the Second World War, it is not really surprising that a majority came to adopt conservative, indeed reactionary, educational policies. There was always a lively minority of dissent, but R. H.

[113]

Tawney, for example, whose writings between the wars were probably the most important single influence on social issues such as equality, was nevertheless by no means an unqualified partisan of the common school for all children. During the war years R. A. Butler, the Minister of Education, appointed a committee to inquire into the question of secondary school curricula after the war. Sir Cyril Norwood, Master of St John's College, Oxford, was chairman, and the committee's report, published in the summer of 1943, began by assuming that there were three broad types of ability for which it would be possible to devise a school system suited to each. The new educational system that was to be planned should take account of this division of ability by the organization of a tripartite structure of grammar school, modern school and technical school. For the first two years there should be as much similarity as possible in the subjects taught in order that if 'mistakes' had been made at the original selection (at age eleven) it would be possible to transfer children at thirteen.

Educational history is well documented. What happened after the Labour victory of 1945 was that the Ministry of Education carried through without basic change the principles of the Norwood report, raised the school leaving age to fifteen in 1947, and increased the total of money for school education. There were many minor improvements, including the schools meal service and free milk, but education was subject to capital cuts, equal pay for women teachers was not achieved and, above all, the degrading and socially divisive eleven-plus selection meant that the majority of working-class children continued to be educated with much inferior facilities than those in the grammar schools, with the opportunities for further education seriously curtailed. The opposition within the Labour movement grew steadily through the second half of the 1940s and by 1951 the Labour Party was committed for the first time to the comprehensive school. By this time the Conservative Party was on the threshold of power for the next thirteen years; and the class divisions in education, established and embedded by the Attlee administration, continued to harden. Moreover, the

Labour Government had ignored the question of the public schools and had left the university structure more or less as it was before the war. The opportunities for a democratic educational system had never been envisaged or understood by the majority of the Labour movement, and British education continued along its conservative and inefficient paths, contributing its full share to an increasingly inefficient society, and, it must be stressed, to the declining radicalism of the British people after 1950.

The Labour Government began to lose its nerve during the second half of 1947. One of the worst winters of the century had led to the fuel crisis; acquiescence in the American Loan agreement about sterling convertibility resulted in a financial crisis in July–August resolved only by the suspension of convertibility after just over a month; and a number of the leading figures in the Government began to show very marked signs of stress and strain. Morrison suffered a thrombosis in the early part of the year and Bevin, so central to the policies of the Government, was steadily deteriorating in health. When he had been examined in 1943 his doctor reported not a sound organ in his body, apart from his feet. He later described Bevin 'comprehensively, as suffering from angina pectoris, cardiac failure, arterio-scelerosis, sinusitis, enlarged liver, damaged kidneys and high blood pressure. He was overweight, smoked and drank more than was good for him, took no exercise and was a poor sleeper'.[15] At the beginning of this crisis year of 1947 Hugh Dalton – who was to be removed from the Exchequer later in the year for a very minor, if foolish, indiscretion – wrote to Attlee on 20 January setting out in sharp terms one of the central contradictions of the Government's policy and one which, as indicated above, was to undermine much of the administration's social policies and intentions. The occasion was a bitter division of opinion within the cabinet on manpower problems and the problem of overseas commitments. Dalton quotes in his memoirs the memorandum he sent to Attlee:

I had already stated in a recent paper to my colleagues that this year 'we cannot afford either the money or the men, for which the Minister of Defence asks . . . We are vainly trying, in every sector of the national economy, to do more than we can. Unless we relax, the result will be rupture. We must think of our national defence, in these hard and heavy years of transition, not only against the more distant possibility of armed aggression, but also against the far more immediate risk of economic and financial overstrain and collapse . . .'

What shall it profit Britain to have even 1,500,000 men in the Forces and Supply, and to be spending nearly £1,000 millions a year on them, if we come to an economic and financial cropper two years hence? . . .

And I am told in Cabinet that to have only 1,400,000 Service and Supply personnel and to spend only £750 millions on them is 'unilateral disarmament'.[16]

By the beginning of 1948 all the major legislation in the Labour Party's programme had been passed, with the exception of the nationalization of iron and steel; and this was a measure which was to arouse very considerable opposition. All the previous nationalization proposals – coal, transport, gas and electricity – had been opposed in principle, but not seriously. Steel, however, was a different proposition. Unlike coal and the railways, iron and steel companies were making profits and the Tories in parliament were by now a much more effective opposition. The industry's trade union leaders were lukewarm; two Labour MPs made public speeches against the Bill when it was published; and senior civil servants were 'unhappy', which meant that they were hostile and certain to be obstructive. There was an illuminating letter from the Government's Chief Planning Officer, Sir Edwin Plowden, who wrote to Stafford Cripps describing the Bill as 'an act of economic irresponsibility' and underlining the risk of upsetting the Americans (some of whom were under the illusion that the Labour Government was introducing socialism to Britain), which would not be wise, Plowden suggested, at a time when Britain was 'dependent upon United States charity'.

The growing hostility to the Labour Government from the

middle and upper classes deserves further emphasis. It was not a working-class phenomenon. Full employment and the introduction of welfare services sustained a working-class support for Labour, as the two elections of 1950 and 1951 were to demonstrate; but among the higher-income groups political apoplexy was developing fast. Their main complaints, among many, derived from the continuation of wartime controls, and with the shortage of domestic servants, the restrictions over foreign travel and food rationing, it was not difficult to persuade the middle classes that Labour was the enemy and that they would do much better under their traditional friends, the Conservative Party. For one thing, of course, the removal of basic controls would ensure that those that have, to them it should be given, a basic tenet of bourgeois society well appreciated by those who have benefited from its operations.

Angela Thirkell was a contemporary novelist, at the bottom end of the second class, with a series of postwar books that were enormously popular, both in Britain and in America. She was the daughter of J. W. Mackail, the biographer of William Morris, and the granddaughter of Burne-Jones, and her writings reflected simply and accurately the frustrations and feelings of the postwar middle classes. The resentment against what she called the Brave New Revolting World found absurd if eloquent expression in her novels; and her middle-class readers, by the thousands, did not, it must be presumed, believe it to be caricature. As one of her female characters in *Private Enterprise* (1947) said: 'What I really mind is their trying to burst up the *Empire* . . . I mean like leaving Egypt and trying to give Gibraltar to the natives. If they try to do anything to Gibraltar, I shall put on a striped petticoat and a muslin fichu and murder them all in their baths, because TRAITORS ought to be murdered'; and while Mrs Thirkell normally treated foreigners, intellectuals and working-class people as figures of fun, she had one academic intellectual adding his learning to the discussion: 'What is interesting, though I must say even to a philosopher damnably galling and uncomfortable, is that we are living under a Government as bad as any in history in its combination of bullying and weakness, its bid for the mob's suffrages, its fawning upon unfriendly foreigners who despise it, its efforts to crush all personal freedom.'

Angela Thirkell's hysterics were made flesh with the formation and activities of the Housewives League; but much more important was the gathering opposition at Westminster, in the City and in business circles in general. John Freeman, who entered Parliament in 1945, later explained in the *New Statesman* (14 November 1959) how the Tories coped with their unexpected and resounding electoral defeat:

It is interesting to recall their subsequent parliamentary strategy. The opposition front bench was not filled up with face-less place men of the 1922 Committee. Alongside Churchill and Eden were to be seen day after day some of the ablest men in Britain . . . all personally appointed by Churchill with orders, after the briefest period of honeymoon which tactical expediency dictated, to attack all the time. I have not forgotten the tension of rising to answer questions or conduct a debate under the cold, implacable eyes of that row of well-tailored tycoons, who hated the Labour government with a passion and fear which made them dedicated men to get it out of office and to limit the damage it could do to the world which they saw as theirs by right . . .

The astonishing re-birth of the Tories and of Tory policy between 1945 and 1950 was not due only to the aggressiveness of the opposition front bench, it was due to their determination to 'limit the damage', to protect their vested interests in their world . . . they had no doubt about the strategic bastions of their system which must be defended at all costs if their future lines of advance were to be kept open. On what they regarded as the vital essentials – containing nationalisation, preserving in office of the personnel of the Establishment, perpetuating the American alliance – they threw in every resource they could command in parliament, the public service, industry and the press.

These are words that could never be written about any Labour opposition at any time in the twentieth century. But the Labour Party after 1945 was in power, and it had the resources of government to counter the propaganda of the Tories in the country; except that they were never used. The Conservative front bench was constantly attacking the Government's information services, and in October 1948 the Labour Government actually appointed a committee to suggest possible economies; and when economies were suggested, the recommendations were carried through. And all this in the closing years of the Labour Government when business and commerce were expending increasing sums of money in advertisements and propaganda against further nationalization and Labour policy in general. It would not have occurred to the Labour leaders to go on the offensive in the country because parliamentarians do not engage in such activity: in office and only occasionally out of office. It had been characteristic of the Labour leadership in the 1930s that opposition was limited to Westminster, and only on very unusual occasions was this self-denying ordnance broken. Certainly it would not be used by a Labour Party in government. The 'national' interest must be served: a central tenet of parliamentarianism as traditionally understood by the Labour socialists of the twentieth century. Thus Chuter Ede, the Home Secretary in the Attlee Government, was responsible for the work of the Boundary Commission which was revising parliamentary constituencies, and which did their work so effectively that thirty seats lost by Labour in 1950 were put down to the skill of the Boundary Commissioners in redrawing constituencies to include additional Conservative voters.

After the general election of February 1950 the Labour majority in the Commons was between five and seven, excluding the Speaker and the Irish Nationalists, who rarely attended. Twenty months later there was another general election and although Labour polled just under 14 million votes – the largest absolute vote so far achieved by any Party – the vagaries of the electoral system gave the Tories a smallish but workable majority in the Commons. In between these two elections Labour continued to add to the reasons why the next thirty years were to be such a miserable record of incompetence and internal discord. The alliance with the

United States was further developed with the outbreak of the Korean War in the summer of 1950; the number of American bases in Britain continued to grow quite rapidly; and a government of tired and sick leaders began to fall apart. Stafford Cripps resigned from the position of Chancellor of the Exchequer in October 1950, and Gaitskell succeeded him; Bevin was finally pushed out in early March 1951 and he died a month later, to be succeeded by Herbert Morrison as Foreign Secretary, and Attlee himself was in hospital for three weeks over the Easter period. Morrison had only seven months in office as Secretary of State but he quickly exhibited the strong imperialist flavour which appears to be an essential element in the make-up of Labour politicians in the twentieth century, especially when they are in office. But the decision which throws the strongest light on the politics of the Labour leadership, and which was uncritically accepted by them in the years which followed, was the announcement by Attlee of a defence expenditure of £3,600 million for 1951–4, a figure which was raised to £4,700 million in January 1951. Britain was already spending 6 per cent of gross national product upon defence; the new estimates increased the percentage to 10 per cent. The American Government and the British Chiefs of Staff had been pressing for £6,000 million or 14 per cent of GNP. Gaitskell introduced the rearmament budget in April 1951. It allowed for an increase in military spending of over £500 million in the year 1951–2 – out of a total of nearly £1,500 million – offset by higher income tax, an increase in the petrol tax, the suspension of investment allowances to industry and charges on false teeth and spectacles under the NHS. It was the last which led to the resignation of Nye Bevan, Harold Wilson and John Freeman. The cancellation of investment allowances exhibited the lack of understanding common to British politicians of all parties concerning the dynamic factors in economic growth. Indeed, this whole rearmament programme, and the high proportion of national resources devoted to defence expenditure, was a further illustration of the economic illiteracy of the British establishment – which included the Labour leadership in the postwar years – and which stemmed from a combination of factors including the great power thesis and the acceptance of a client status in relation to American foreign policy. What was missed, and missed totally in these years, were the consequences for the British economy of such high levels of expenditure on arms and overseas military commitments.

Gaitskell's budget was well received by most of the Parliamentary Labour Party but before its full implications could be worked out Attlee decided upon a further general election. When the Tories returned to office they found they had to reduce the levels of defence spending agreed by the Labour Government. Attlee was asked at the time why he had gone for an early election when there was no obvious reason for the decision. 'Because I thought it was time to declare,' said Attlee. The young candidate who had asked the question had clearly never thought of politics in cricketing images, but he replied: 'I don't think they play by the same rules,' to which Attlee answered 'we shall get another innings in some day if we don't win this time'. The reasons behind Attlee's decision were that he and his colleagues were morally and politically bankrupt. Labour socialism had arrived at a dead end. There was nothing left of the radical assumptions which had shaped the Labour Party's policies in 1945. Their ideas on the future of British society were empty of serious content; their basic premises were now much enfeebled, and there was no way forward from their current policies; nor was there to be in the years to come.[17]

6
The wasted years: 1951–79

The dominating fact of twentieth-century Britain has been a marked relative decline in world power relations, much accelerated after the Second World War. It was, of course, inevitable that Britain could not retain her economic dominance of the Victorian period, but the main cause for the sharpness of the decline has been the inefficiency of British manufacturing production in the twentieth century, and the failure to adjust quickly enough to changing structures of world trade. Paradoxically, victory in two world wars assisted the falling away of Britain as a significant force in world affairs, and this was especially true of the aftermath of 1945. Victory meant that there was no strong pressure to recast and reorganize a society that was suffering from the clogging effects of many vested interests, and again especially after 1945 the long secular boom meant that the propertied classes and their political representatives have continued to strengthen their position within domestic politics. Moreover, the considerable part which Britain played in the defeat of Fascism encouraged a range of myths concerning Britain's position in the postwar world that was now unfolding. Pierson Dixon, a career official in the Foreign Office who became Ernest Bevin's private secretary, having served

Anthony Eden in the same capacity, wrote in his diary of Bevin's 'wholly delightful assumption that of the three [USA, Russia and Britain] we were still the biggest'. What Dixon ought to have written was that it ranked among the more unfortunate of Bevin's many illusions concerning the postwar world.

It is certainly true that at the end of the war Britain was one of the richest countries, much further ahead than the war-shattered economies of Europe. Only those who had remained neutral, Sweden and Switzerland, had higher per capita incomes than Britain; but it was only a decade or so after the war that Britain's economic weaknesses began to be apparent. By 1979 the British gross national product was not much more than half her immediate neighbours' in western Europe; and in manufacturing the Thatcher administration has achieved an accelerating process of decline since 1979. Output in manufacturing fell by 14 per cent between 1979 and 1983, and although there has been a slight improvement in the most recent years, the general crisis of these years has only been covered by the very large surpluses generated from North Sea oil and gas. In the early 1980s Britain was around seventeenth in the world league of gross national product per head.[1]

The problems of the British economy have been maturing for over a century. In the Paris Exhibition of 1867 there was already quite a wide-ranging criticism of British goods which produced the first of many reports on the backward state of technical training for industry. It has not been documentation that the British lacked, for down to the outbreak of the Second World War there was an abundance of detailed information on the low levels of most manufacturing and mining industries; the result of inadequate investment, poor quality management and bitter industrial relations, whether expressed openly or harboured. When J. T. Murphy, one of the militant engineering shop stewards of the First World War, re-entered his trade at a large works in London in the summer of 1940 – and this was after two decades – he found that his lathe was of the same type as he had used twenty years earlier, that the pace of work was

[123]

slow, that management were distant from the workers, that workers were as suspicious as ever of management's intentions and that shop-steward control of the factory floor was tight. Shop-floor experience during the Second World War, when publicity of these matters was more common, disclosed innumerable stories of inefficiency and incompetence; and this evidence was abundantly confirmed in the official reports that began to accumulate as the end of the war approached.

A Ministry of Reconstruction was established in March 1943, and most of the work on postwar industrial matters was delegated to various subcommittees which largely used information gathered on industrial sectors by the Board of Trade. This was Hugh Dalton's ministry, and there flooded into his office and into those other ministries also concerned with production and exports a devastating picture of industrial backwardness, above all in the traditional export industries of iron and steel, cotton and coal. Comparisons made later between Britain and German industries during the war confirmed that in almost all cases the productivity of the latter outstripped, and often greatly exceeded, the former. The Spitfire, for example, was as effective a fighting machine as the Messerschmitt 109, but it took some two-thirds more man-hours to build than the German plane. The production of tanks during the war was an utterly dismal story that foreshadowed the wholly justified complaints about British cars in the postwar years. One of the central problems for the wartime production of tanks was the small size and technical inefficiency of the design departments of the many different firms involved. Far too many firms, it should be added; and compared with German firms the British were not only poor in design but were inefficient in product development with a technology that was outdated. All these matters, let it be noted, were the responsibility of management, and their industrial illiteracy during wartime was made worse by the bureaucracies of the military and the War Office who rarely knew their own minds in the matter of specifications, and kept changing what they thought they knew.[2]

The civil servants who advised the Labour administration

after 1945 on commercial and industrial questions knew all these things – one must assume that they read their own reports – and a number of Labour ministers had also been closely involved within the coalition Government. It is interesting that Dalton, in his published memoirs, makes no reference to these problems during the period when he was at the Board of Trade: although his own reports and comments can be read in cabinet and other departmental papers; and it is further interesting that his biographer – in a highly instructive volume – also says nothing about this part of Dalton's work at the Board of Trade. Both, it may be suggested, are an indication of the continued failure to appreciate the quite crucial nature of this problem for the Attlee administration and for the future development of the British economy throughout the whole of the postwar period. The issues involved were underlined once again with the series of reports published in the later years of the Attlee Government from teams of industrialists, trade unionists and civil servants who went to study a range of industrial questions in the United States, and provide a comparative analysis with Britain. These Anglo-American reports on productivity exhibited once more the low levels of industrial performance on the British side of the Atlantic, but again their impact upon political opinion was remarkably limited. The high level of world demand for British goods after 1945, and the fast rate of growth of exports – wartime controls still continued to restrict consumption and imports – contributed to the disregard, which in many cases was ignorance, of the underlying problems of the British economy. It was the fact of full employment and the strong growth of production that bedazzled – the word is not too strong – the Government, their civil servants and the mainstream Labour intellectuals.

John Strachey is a case in point. Before 1939 he had been an important influence on the Marxist and the Marxisant left, but was already shifting to a Labour-type Keynesianism by the time the war began. He served as a junior minister in the Attlee administrations, and in the postwar years became a not unimportant intellectual influence, although never as influential as Crosland. Strachey wrote the concluding chapter in *New*

Fabian Essays (1952), a seminal document of the 1950s. In 'The Tasks and Achievements of British Labour' he set out the main statistics of industrial growth, and of exports, between 1938 and 1950. Most of the increases had occurred after 1945, and Strachey went on to pose the question which for his generation of Labour socialists was central to their thinking: 'what has been done to the old, staid – indeed stagnant – British economy to make it behave in this way? Was it really the measures of the Labour Government which wrought this remarkable change? And if so, which measures?' The answer that Strachey gave to his question, broadly accepted by his fellow Labour intellectuals, was that the full employment of the postwar years was the result of the development of democratic and effective institutions which permitted representative government to be genuinely responsive to people's needs. Keynesianism provided the techniques of government economic management. Strachey noted that full employment was also present in the United States, but he insisted that the 'major factor' in the achievement of these postwar changes 'must always be the shift in social and political power by which alone forces which even *want* to run the economy at full speed may come to the controls. Without that shift no mere economic techniques can have any effect'.

Strachey's comment about the 'old, staid – indeed stagnant – British economy' of pre-1939 days was wholly typical of his generation. They were all dominated in their thinking by unemployment, depressed areas and the hunger marches which were now the symbol of those prewar years. What remained in their minds was the poverty, which was indeed widespread, and the Conservative social policies, which were harsh and uncaring, and here their thinking stopped. What they did not appreciate was that, with all the many problems of the British economy and its failure to restructure itself away from the traditional export sectors of the years before 1914, the 1930s was a period of economic growth, in spite of the fact that even in the best year of the decade unemployment never fell below one million. But manufacturing production increased by one-third between 1929 and 1937, and this in spite of the sharp decline of the crisis years between 1930 and 1932. By comparison with other capitalist societies of the 1930s Britain was emphatically not stagnant. It is true that there were significant indications of a further downturn in 1938, but that is another matter and Britain then began to move into an armaments-based economy. After 1945, and especially after 1950, world developments were to falsify Strachey's central argument; that for dynamic change what was first needed was 'a real change in the balance of the social system'. Japan was only one of many capitalist societies that illustrated the mistakes of the argument. As already remarked upon above, it was Crosland in *The Future of Socialism* who developed the Strachey thesis into a general argument about the changed nature of capitalism in the postwar period. As Crosland wrote in his concluding section in the republished version of 1964; 'The level of material welfare will soon be such that marginal changes in the allocation of resources will make little difference to anyone's contentment': a staggering piece of rigmarole for the 1950s, when it was first written, as for the 1960s.

Most of the contributors to *New Fabian Essays* were to become the next generation of Labour leaders or the intellectual influence upon those leaders, and in general they provided the intellectual baggage, such as it was, during the long years of Conservative Government. In 1951 when the Labour Party gained their highest ever vote but lost their majority in the House of Commons, they found themselves in a society which was certainly not prepared to go back to the days before 1939. The world boom ensured that full employment would continue, and with a strongly defensive Labour movement the Tories had no alternative but to leave the social legislation of the Attlee administration more or less intact. What did not happen was any serious thinking on the part of the Labour leadership, or the intellectuals of the movement, concerning the measures required for the further development of a more socially progressive society. In part, as we have seen, this was the consequence of a grossly over-blown and utterly mistaken analysis of what had been accomplished since 1945, for which Crosland and the *New*

Fabian essayists were responsible. More important, perhaps, was the fact of continued full employment with the resultant rise in living standards, and the inability of the intellectuals of the left to comprehend what was happening to the world capitalist system. For the British economy, the 1950s were crucial. The under-investment in industry that had been endemic in most sectors in the years between the wars, now continued with the easy world market conditions of the 1950s. It was not until the payments crisis of the early 1960s that the nature of the new competitive world became obvious even to the British. By this time the problems of the economy – low levels of investment, inadequate and incompetent managerial skills in the manufacturing sector, the poor quality of engineering and technological training, a strongly entrenched trade unionism in a number of key sectors – all combined to produce the conditions for a level of growth much lower than its competitors. And the lower levels of growth were associated, in a number of industrial groups, with declining rates of profit that induced even lower investment for the future. The abolition of physical controls, already begun in the closing years of the Attlee administration, and the rapid restoration of Treasury control, meant the defence of sterling whatever the consequences for the manufacturing sector, and contributed to the policies of 'stop–go' and the persistence of Britain's economic decline relative to her obvious competitors. A major factor in Britain's weak economic performance, still greatly underestimated to the present day, has been the high levels of defence expenditure – measured in relation to gross national product – with the accompanying effects of grossly distorted scientific and technological research.

All this had passed the Labour leadership by. In 1955 the Labour Party for the first time in its history elected a professional economist as its leader, and his lack of awareness of the structural weaknesses of the British economy may be taken as a tribute to an intellectual discipline that has been disastrously unhelpful in the past forty years. So what were the concerns of the Labour leadership during the 1950s? The closing months of the second Attlee Government had been dominated by the growing split between the majority of the cabinet and those around Aneurin Bevan, following the latter's resignation over Gaitskell's budget in the spring of 1951. The next few years – indeed many years – were much involved with the bitter conflict between right and left. Gaitskell emerged as the leading political figure for the succession to Attlee from the time of the Morecambe Conference of 1952, and Attlee continued in place as leader until 1955 in order to defeat the pretensions of Herbert Morrison for the position, and thereby ensure that Gaitskell was successful.

Gaitskell was not a particularly good tactician, but he had all the qualities required by the right wing of the Party and the trade union leadership; and he was sustained throughout his career, with only one exceptional year, by the block vote of the right-wing trade unions. He helped to contain the Bevanites, to defeat them over the issue of German rearmament in 1954, and in all matters of fundamental policy Gaitskell was an enthusiastic and undeviating supporter of the American alliance. He was bitterly anti-Communist and as firmly anti-Soviet as any member of the American Government could wish. He had nothing to offer in terms of domestic policy for the Labour Party except a general watering down of the commitments to public ownership that were among the staple items of traditional Labour socialism; and it was evidence of his tactical incompetence that he fought the issue. But above all, in the closing period of his life, he kept the independent nuclear bomb for the British people.

What the historian of the future will make of the Labour leadership in the 1950s is an interesting question. Its ineffectiveness as an opposition was, of course, nothing new. So it had been in the 1930s and so it was to be again during the Thatcher years. But in the 1950s there were certain differences from what had gone before. Above all, this was the first period in the history of the modern Labour movement, except for the years of the First World War, that the Labour leadership in Parliament was in more or less complete accord with the Tory Government on the fundamentals of foreign and colonial policies. Gaitskell and the right of the Labour movement vigorously supported a high level of rearmament because that was what their anti-Sovietism involved, and most important, that was what the American alliance considered central to their agreements. It should be noted that these included an increasing number of American bases in the United Kingdom, including nuclear installations, with no control over their use in a military crisis, or what was considered to be a military crisis. In the final analysis the finger on the trigger was the finger of the President of the United States.[3] These were not, however, questions with which the Labour parliamentary opposition considered it necessary to bother the Government; nor was there any discussion of the economic consequences of rearmament for the British economy. What was crucial was the maintenance of the British independent bomb, representing perhaps 1 per cent of the nuclear strike of the two super-powers. It was a decision that was not only wholly misguided but must be characterized as pathetic; but not to Gaitskell and his colleagues. Just as Dalton kept his strongest language for the dissidents of 1939, so Gaitskell engaged in fighting words of a kind that he never used against his Tory opponents. It was his final speech before the Labour Party Conference of 1960, when the motion for unilateralism was carried, that contained the famous peroration: 'We will fight and fight and fight again to bring back sanity and honesty and dignity, so that our Party with its great past may retain its glory and its greatness.' As Denis Healey remarked, Gaitskell 'always felt that he was fighting for the right, not only against people who were mistaken, but who were immorally mistaken'.

It has always been thus, of course; the gods and their moralities are so often invoked in quite indiscriminate ways. And while the atom bomb was the central issue of the postwar world there were many other aspects of foreign policy, and especially colonial policy, on which the Labour leadership offered no independent stance but were concerned, in all fundamentals, to follow the Tories. What Bevin began or continued – in Greece, Palestine, Indo-China, Indonesia, Malaysia and above all in reinforcement of the Americans' Korean War – his successors in the Labour leadership supported Tory policy concerning the almost continuous series of colonial wars that ran through the decade of the 1950s and the early 1960s. Mau Mau and Kenya, British Guiana, Cyprus and Aden were among the now tattered parts of the British Empire that spilled a great deal of blood before independence or something approaching independence was achieved. The later 1960s and the 1970s saw the crisis of what is now Zimbabwe; the 1970s Northern Ireland; and the 1980s the Falklands. Only at the time of the Suez aggression was the Labour leadership in total opposition; but so were the Americans. As remarked earlier, radical movements in Britain have not only opposed the domestic policies of the Conservatives, but there has always been a criticism – and usually a vigorous criticism – of foreign or colonial policies. It has apparently never occurred to the Labour leadership of this postwar period that collaboration on foreign affairs has consistently weakened its opposition on domestic matters; and there is no question but that Labour opposition in the House of Commons since 1951 has been lamentable in its effeteness and incompetence; reaching its nadir during the period of the first Thatcher administration, from 1979 to the almost unbelievable ineptness of the 1983 general election campaign.

The history of the 1960s and the 1970s, which saw two periods of Labour Government – from 1964 to 1970, and from 1974 to 1979 – do not require any detailed chronology. There was just one period when a new advance might have taken place. Harold Wilson appeared to offer a new beginning to the Labour Party when he became leader in 1963, following Gaitskell's death. He told the Labour Party Conference, in words which have been much quoted, that the new Britain he was planning would be 'forged in the white heat' of a scientific revolution in which there would be no place 'for restrictive practices or out-dated methods on either side of industry'. When he won a bare majority in October 1964 he set in motion a number of reforms, among them a new Department of Economic Affairs that would be responsible for promoting long-term growth on the basis of a National Five-Year Plan. The clear intention was to curtail the power of the Treasury and its preoccupation with short-term policies in keeping down Government expenditure and maintaining the value of sterling. There was also some recognition of the need to encourage industrial investment as well as the modernization of the state apparatus.

When Wilson called a general election in the spring of 1966, his majority increased to ninety-six; but the hopes he had encouraged – and these included some sections of industry – were quickly disappointed. For one thing, the Minister in charge of the Department of Economic Affairs was George Brown, already a near alcoholic and intellectually well below his new responsibilities. More important was the continuation of the old policies of heavy overseas commitments, massive efforts to prop up sterling – the flight from which began in earnest after the first Labour budget – and the continuous failure to recognize the crucial weaknesses in the manufacturing sector. Social reform, already promised, was held back, and the attempts to impose a wage curb ended in disaster. From 1969 the number of working days lost in strikes escalated steadily to a new postwar record of 23.9 million in 1972; and the performance of government throughout the 1970s continued along the same lines, compounded by the world crisis which followed the massive increase in oil prices in 1973–4. The movement of capital abroad accelerated during the Conservative Government of Edward Heath between 1970 and 1974; and the minority Labour Governments from 1974 to 1979, first under Wilson and then Callaghan, failed totally to solve anything except by agreement with the International Monetary Fund on the need to cut back government expenditures. Inflation rose to 26 per cent over the twelve months from July 1975 to July 1976; unemployment was rising and deindustrialization becoming more marked; and the Labour administration of Callaghan ended in a winter of discontent when the number of working days lost exceeded those of 1972 by over 5 million.

The Labour years of the 1960s and 1970s were not without some social advances, although the continued rise of living standards was still largely the result of the continuation of full, or nearly full employment. The Wilson administration to 1970 provided increased expenditure on a range of social services and the first Race Relations Acts were passed; but the latter were very slow to make any serious impact upon the growing problem of racism, and the former left untouched the existing distribution of wealth, income and social privilege. After 1974 there was put on the statute-book trade union legislation which provided important procedural rights of employed workers, including improved maternity leave for most women workers. Nevertheless, by their incompetent handling of the economy, the attempts to impose wage discipline upon an unchanged industrial system and the absence of anything close to an imaginative approach to the changing problems of British society the Labour administration steadily alienated its own constituency. In the general election of May 1979 there was a massive swing of 2.2 million votes to the Conservatives, including an 8 per cent swing among skilled industrial workers. This 1979 election marked the end of a thirty-year period during which the Labour movement in general has slowly but inexorably fragmented the diffuse radical consciousness which gave the Labour Party nearly 14 million votes in 1951, most of them, let it be remembered, from among the working-class electorate. It became obvious in 1979 that the gap between leaders and led had widened steadily, and the intellectual and political emptiness of those nominally offering leadership was starkly revealed; as it was to be even more bleakly exhibited in the years which followed.[4]

The explanation of complex historical phenomena is never simple, and always problematic in the analysis of their many different parts; but there are certain characteristics of the postwar Labour movement that in the context of this present study require further emphasis. One is the notable absence of new developments in socialist thinking. We can disregard Crosland, whose main emphasis – once the inadequacy of his economic understanding is put aside – was upon equality and the development of individual freedom. These are matters which no one disputes, and indeed it is proper and meet that each generation of socialists should redefine their meaning

[133]

for their own lives. But equality was hardly a new theme; and the real problem was not the acceptance of equality as a basic principle of socialist strategy but the manner of its achievement. And this, when the Labour Party came to power, failed dismally to provide even the first steps towards that more equal society which has been the inspiration of socialists since socialism as an idea and as a movement first appeared. But what has been striking about the decades since 1945 has been the remarkable paucity of ideas about what a future socialist society would imply for its citizens. In part this has been the result of the mistaken understanding of what the Attlee administrations actually achieved and the absence of any serious challenge to the ideas of the Fabian revisionists in the 1950s. In part, too, it has been the difficulty which the socialist intellectuals of Britain – and of western Europe in general – have shown in coming to terms with the relative affluence of sections of working people and the long secular boom in the world economy; as if the possession of a house or flat, a family car and holidays abroad are incompatible with a continued revulsion against the greed and moral decadence of the post-war world, expressed not least in the deepening crisis of those 'damned of the earth' who live in what is known as the Third World. There is another matter to be considered. The impact of Stalinism in the Soviet Union and the countries of eastern Europe has been profound in western Europe and other areas of affluence in the world. This is not to suggest that the implications of Stalinism have not been world-wide, but simply underlines the influence it has had upon the working-class and socialist movements of the industrially advanced world, given the extraordinary power which the 1917 Revolution exercised upon them. West European socialists and Marxists have found it difficult to elaborate new ideas and new concepts. What has eluded them has been the relationship between social ownership, central planning and individual freedom; and in the wider popular consciousness it has been the absence of civil liberties in regimes that have styled themselves socialist that has been the most important single handicap in the creation of a vision of a socialist project that would take hold of the imagination of ordinary people.

There are, however, in this context, certain paradoxes to be noted. While the 1950s was a dull and conservative decade in Britain, the following twenty years saw a considerable growth of interest in Marxism, and this within some general changes of ideas which reached their peak in the student discontent of 1968. Such changes were not always radical, even in a broad political sense, and some were self-interested indulgences; but it was now possible to speak of an implantation of Marxism in British intellectual life. It was, and remains, however, a notably narrow influence, a result in some part of the unfortunate fact that theoretical rigour in Marxist terms can apparently only be achieved by many authors in a density of language comprehensible only to the few, but much more because of the failure to engage in sustained polemic with the dominant ideas of the time. There have been exceptions, of course, but the basic problems of British society were only slowly recognized and systematically analysed. The New Left, which as an intellectual movement developed rapidly during 1956 following the secret speech of Khrushchev, Suez and the Soviet invasion of Hungary, continued to make a considerable impact in succeeding years; but its longer-term influence has been a good deal less than might have been expected. There are today proportionately more socialists in Britain than at any previous period, in large part the consequences of the New Left of the late 1950s and of the generation of 1968, and the bookshelves are bursting with socialist volumes, tracts and pamphlets. And yet the social consciousness of workers in trade unions is less radical than it was in the immediate aftermath of the war, and the left, in any of its manifestations, has been unable to sustain a political grouping of any significance outside the membership of the Labour Party.

For the first time in the twentieth century there is no political organization of any importance to the left of the Labour Party that is developing a distinctive socialist perspective and at the same time developing the organizational channels to transmit ideas and policies into the main bodies of the Labour movement. This is what the ILP and the Social Democratic Federation achieved before 1914 and the Communist Party, with conspicuous success, in the 1930s. This absence of a left grouping outside the Labour Party has set new problems for socialists, and the decline of the Communist Party and of the *gauchiste* parties and groups during the last decade and a half has inevitably encouraged a proliferation of single-issue organizations concerned with specific questions. Such bodies have always been part of the British political scene, but the steady attrition of the organized left has undoubtedly enhanced their importance.

The Campaign for Nuclear Disarmament has been by far the most important of the single-issue campaigns and it has had a considerable impact upon public opinion,[5] in spite of certain particular disadvantages. One disadvantage has been the absence of an anti-war consciousness of the kind that developed so strongly in Britain in the late 1920s and the 1930s. The First World War was a traumatic experience for the British people, whereas the evocation of the Second World War is still, forty years later, of the 'gung-ho' approach. Allied with this has been the widespread sentiment of anti-Communism and especially anti-Sovietism and the deep-rooted popular belief in the inherent expansionism of the Russian regime. This is one of the reasons – there are others – why the anti-nuclear movement has mostly not directly related itself to fundamental issues of foreign policy, and also no doubt why the movement diminished almost to insignificance between the middle 1960s and the mid 1970s, reviving strongly from about 1977–8. There have been other single-issue movements of importance, above all connected with the rediscovery of poverty in the late 1950s. However, the most critical development of the postwar era has been the emergence of feminism: a movement whose potential for fundamental social change is still in its very early stages.[6]

There have always been socialist feminists within the British Labour movement, and before 1914 the Co-operative Women's Guild was an important pioneering organization which continued throughout the interwar years; and there was a slow growth of commitment to women's emancipation. But the feminism of the post-1960 years was of a different order from anything that had gone before, and in Britain the Labour Party and the trade unions have been distinctly backward in accepting the very large implications of the new demands for sexual equality. Their failure to appreciate the political and social possibilities of the liberation of women from centuries of subordination and dependence was part of the general bankruptcy of ideas that has been so dispiriting, a narrowing of the vision of what a more egalitarian society could mean for the lives of ordinary people, and a failure to comprehend the new potentialities of industrial society in the age of high technology. It was this lack of imagination about the future that made the very modest achievements of the Greater London Council under Ken Livingstone in the 1980s appear so much more significant than they really were. At the very least a part of the movement was standing firm against the hysteria of much of the media, and it was showing some enterprise in the projects it was supporting. By contrast the national leadership was dull, uninspired and too often, after 1979, demoralized.

One of the many intellectual failures of the left in the past quarter of a century has been the inability of socialist writers and critics to come to terms with the leading ideas of their age. There are some obvious names that provide the exceptions, but the generalization holds. Take the historians, for example. The first intellectual discipline to develop a serious Marxist approach in Britain was the work of the young Communist Party historians in the decade after 1945; and their writings up to the present day have been wide-ranging and influential. But if one takes the publications of Marxist historians working in the modern period – from early industrialization to our own day – it is striking how much effort has gone into the history of the working class in Britain, and how little into the power and politics of the ruling classes. It was, no doubt, the outstanding influence of Eric Hobsbawm and Edward Thompson which helped to encourage this emphasis, and in any case it is accepted that the history of past radical movements is or should be an essential part of the political education of contemporary radicals and socialists. History from below was largely unploughed territory and the work of the past thirty years has made much more vivid, and more relevant, the landscape of the past in which the

[137]

common people lived and worked. But it has to be noted that the majority of radically minded or Marxist historians who work in the modern period concentrate largely upon nineteenth-century, working-class history, with a special convergence on the radicalism of the pre-1850 decades, and little upon the dominant themes of twentieth-century society, including the economics and politics of appeasement in the 1930s, or the Cold War, in all its many manifestations, after 1945. Without depreciating the considerable scholarship that has been achieved it cannot but be remarked that some, at least, of this interest in the working-class past has a feeling of rather cosy antiquarianism about it.

Political scientists and political economists have begun, in the last decade or so, to remedy the large gaps in the radical-socialist understanding of contemporary Britain, although it was an historian, Eric Hobsbawm, who first drew attention to the steadily weakening Labour consciousness among the working-class electorate.[7] In the 1960s Miliband began the analysis of labourism and of the characteristics of the British state[8] and the following decade saw a steadily increasing flow of analytical literature, with still, however, many areas of social and political life untouched by any radical critique. What has not yet happened is the coming together of the conclusions of a growing literature and the formulation of policies that could sustain a serious movement among the activists of the trade unions and of the Labour Party. There have been attempts. The 'alternative economic strategy' caught the imagination of some groups for a few years but the mainstream of the movement was not seriously influenced; and it is here that the dynamic activity of a left grouping, which could help disseminate ideas and provide the militants with policies to encourage their acceptance, has been missed. What we have, and there could be serious implications when the American experience is considered, is the presence of a socialist intellectual enclave largely, although not wholly, divorced from working people, whether organized or not.

This gap, between the understanding of society by those active socialists in the Labour and trade union movement and the many other parts of the working-class community and, to a lesser extent, of the middle strata, can be illustrated by the history of the trade unions in the past thirty years. Before 1939 there was a positive correlation between trade union membership and Labour voting, and there still is, but it is weakening. In the years before the Second World War it was the unorganized, often the unskilled, often the unemployed, who either voted Tory or abstained, while in the decades since 1945 there has been a steady drift of trade unionists away from the Labour Party, especially accelerated, it would seem, in the 1970s. The political leadership has obviously much to answer for, but the trade union executives have also to accept serious responsibility for these changes in political consciousness. It has always been true that wage militancy has no necessary connection with an advanced political position, and if the unions, the basic defensive mechanisms against the power of capital, restrict themselves to matters of wages and narrowly defined working conditions, then individual self-interest on the part of their ordinary members, and sectionalism in general, will be encouraged. The balance between straight industrial questions and the broader politics of industry is always a shifting one and never easy to define in advance, or to deal with in practice. What can be said of the post-1950 period is that British trade unions have shown themselves notably unimaginative even within the boundaries they have always accepted. Like the Labour leadership, those in commanding positions in the unions have failed, for the most part, to appreciate the growing economic problems of British capitalism, and they have had nothing to offer that would help reverse the worsening living standards of manual workers relative to their opposite numbers in other advanced industrial societies.

Trade union research departments have remained wholly inadequate, and the unions' attitudes towards research have mirrored the intellectual philistinism of their employers. Above all, the unions have failed completely to offset the dismal public image of nationalization. What positive ideas have been current, and they have been few, have largely come from outside bodies, such as the Institute for Workers'

Control, whose own activities flourished for a few years and then declined sharply in the second half of the 1970s. The most imaginative plans for trade union renewal and workers' participation were from the Lucas Combine Committee whose original impetus derived from the threat of large-scale redundancies in the early 1970s, and whose ideas for the conversion of the company's resources into socially useful products were widely discussed and commented on; but not by most of the official trade movement or by the majority of the Labour leadership.

What happened to the Lucas Plan has been a most instructive story and it underlines the narrowness of vision that has afflicted the trade union bureaucracy and their political colleagues.[9] The most serious weakness, let it be said again, has been the failure to understand the potentialities of a dynamic sector of state enterprise which could not only pioneer new techniques of management and workers' participation, but could at the same time act in a sharply competitive way in the open market with private enterprise. There was much that could have been learned from European experience and translated into a British context; but the unions in general, while not as incompetent as those responsible for the retail Co-operative sector – which was almost eliminated from British towns after the 1950s – wholly failed to take advantage of their increased numerical strength and financial resources to make themselves a force for progressive ideas and imaginative action. When, after 1979, confronted with growing unemployment complemented by the bitter and continuous offensive by the Tories against trade unions in general and their legal status in particular, their defences proved fumbling, inefficient and largely ineffective. The shop floor has often shown more resilience than head office.

It was remarked above (p. 68) that, unlike certain other countries of western Europe, there was no radical or revolutionary tradition in England. Ireland, of course, was always different, and Scottish and Welsh nationalism since the Second World War have imparted a somewhat different tone to politics within their own boundaries. But in England there has been a striking absence of a Labour-socialist culture. The

beginnings of a counter-culture to the domination of bourgeois and petty-bourgeois ideas was growing steadily if
slowly in the first half of the twentieth century; but the years
since the Second World War have seen a dwindling and a
decline. There is still political education by the trade unions,
there are lively institutions such as Ruskin and the Northern
College, there are history workshops and socialist festivals;
but the signs of anything approaching a national radical
culture, vibrant, creative and imaginative, are lacking. The
movement which polls millions of electoral votes, even in its
worst years, cannot sustain a daily paper, in a society in
which newspapers are read by the masses in their millions.
And yet there *are* more individual socialists today than ever
before, there is a constant outpouring of socialist literature,
and the response of hundreds of thousands of ordinary
people to the year-long miners' strike in 1984–5 was a
remarkable social and political phenomenon. There are some
crucial paradoxes here to be seriously debated.

The political consensus which emerged during the Attlee
administrations was continued, more or less, by the Conservative Party, and lasted through the next two decades. It then
began to be seriously undermined during the 1970s. The
resurgence of industrial militancy in the late 1960s and early
1970s alarmed the business community at a time when the
long-term decline in the rate of profit was being assessed with
much foreboding. The dramatic rise in oil prices in 1973–4
brought together the elements of crisis in the British
economy: the steady rise in unemployment which by 1979
had reached 1.2 million; the deindustrialization in the manufacturing sector that was to accelerate so sharply after 1979
with the levels of manufactured imports exceeding exports
by 1982–3. The apparent agreement which Labour had relied
upon since 1945 between full employment, rising living
standards and comprehensive social welfare was now at an
end; and the postwar vision of a Labour movement as part of
a 'progressive capitalist' economy had become a mirage.

The political history of the Labour Party since 1945 has
been largely shaped by the decisions taken during the Attlee
administrations between the end of the war and 1951. It has

been a sorry tale. The uneven, diffuse but genuine radicalism of so many of the British people at the end of the war has been largely dissipated, and their historical conservatism in political and social attitudes has now become a good deal more pronounced. The creation of a socialist society was never on the agenda at the end of the war, but radical change was, and it could have continued in the decades which followed, had the movement in the mass been offered policies which stirred their imagination and encouraged their sense of fair-minded collectivity. Instead, there has taken place a steady erosion of radical politics. Britain has remained a highly secretive society and the lack of openness has steadily grown worse under Labour and Tory Governments. The development of new ideas has apparently been beyond the intellectual and political capabilities of the leaders of the Labour movement. The Abortion Act of 1967, the Sexual Offences Act of the same year (as a result of which homosexual relations between consenting adults in private was permitted) and the abolition of capital punishment in 1969 were all passed by a Labour Government, but they were the marks of a civilized society and there was nothing specifically Labour socialist about such measures. What has been more striking has been the steady retreat into conservative attitudes in the 1970s. There has been a civil war in Northern Ireland for about two decades, but at not one of five general elections since British troops moved into the province did the issue become a matter of major public debate and discussion.

It was this impoverishment of Labour socialism that prepared the way for the striking acceptance of the language and the practice of Thatcherism from 1979, and the equally remarkable collapse of any serious opposition by the Labour Party inside Westminster, and by the Party and the trade union movement outside. If the Labour movement returns, as it must, to the pioneering slogans of its early days – educate, agitate, organize – their translation into the idiom of the closing years of the twentieth century will not be achieved in any mechanical way. A radical socialist movement is not only a denial of private and public greed and acquisitiveness; to win mass support it must be sharply intelligent and realistically practical. Above all, it must rest upon the traditional socialist virtues of the harmony of the public good with the good life of the individual and the social group. And that means the achievement of the most difficult of all civic responsibilities: a working accord between liberty and equality.

Epilogue

The Labour movement and the miners' strike: 1984–5

The bitter strike of the British miners began on 12 March 1984, and lasted effectively for nearly a year. It was the largest industrial dispute of the whole postwar period, and the course of events during the strike provides a commentary upon the arguments of this monograph. It must be emphasized at the outset that what follows is not a detailed analysis of the strike from which conclusions about the conduct of the strike by the NUM leadership can be drawn; nor does it offer any examination of the place of coal and the mining industry in a comprehensive energy policy. These are not its purposes. This short account is intended to consider in a selective way some of the problems and the weaknesses revealed during the months of the strike, the purpose of which is to underline certain of the general points made in the preceding chapters. It is based almost entirely upon an earlier and more comprehensive article by the author.[1]

The strike was long premeditated. The general strategy had been laid down in the Ridley Report which was leaked, and published, by *The Economist* on 27 May 1978. The Conservative Party and the business world in general had been deeply disturbed at the actions of the miners in 1972 and 1974 and this led to a marked hardening of attitudes against the miners in particular and unionism in general. When the Tories won the general election of 1979, one of the central items in their policy was the alteration in the legal position of trade unions. Their exceedingly hostile attitude towards the miners was confirmed by the retreat they had to make in February 1981 over pit closures, understood as only temporary. Ian MacGregor was appointed Chairman of the Coal Board in September 1983, and there was no more obvious signal of what was in store for the miners, given his notable success in 'streamlining' the steel industry. In March 1984 the South Yorkshire Coal Board Director announced the closure of Cortonwood colliery, and this was the beginning of a sequence of events that quickly led, not to a national strike, but a strike of both the Yorkshire and Scottish areas that spread to most districts with the notable exception of Nottingham and some adjacent areas. A national ballot was never called, and about 20 per cent of the labour force continued working throughout the strike.

The timing of the strike was not in the miners' interest, as the Coal Board and the NUM knew; but the miners' leadership took on the challenge. The first matter of note is the attitude of the Parliamentary Labour Party. It has been argued above that the PLP, when in opposition, tended to limit their opposition to Westminster, but even in the Commons, in the long travail of the miners' strike, the Labour front bench made very little comment. As the *Guardian* remarked towards the end of the strike, the historian of the future will not go to the pages of *Hansard* for a detailed commentary because it was not in fact a matter of serious concern for the House of Commons, judging by the number of printed columns. There is no doubt that Neil Kinnock, only recently elected leader of the opposition, had some special problems, apart from his own inexperience. Arthur Scargill was a very difficult miners' leader to deal with; the violence on the TV screens every night was certainly due, in part, to the tactics of mass picketing; and above all, the strike lacked the legitimacy of a national ballot: a matter naturally at the centre of the Tory argument. Confronted with these problems, the Labour front bench ran away. During the first ten weeks of the strike, after which the Commons went on holiday for a fortnight, there was no debate initiated by the Labour front bench. David Owen, of the SDP, who expressly stated that he wanted the miners to lose and who throughout the strike exhibited his own conservative attitudes, said on 17 May:

> once again we should be going on holiday without having had a debate on the miners' dispute. In view of the fact that the Opposition, who control totally the opportunities for debate, have not seen fit to allow a debate, will the Leader of the House give a promise to those of us, on both sides of the house I think, who feel that there should be a debate, that he will initiate a debate in Government time immediately after the holiday if the Leader of the Opposition has not plucked up enough courage to have a debate?

There had been debates initiated by back benchers, some of whom showed considerable tenacity in their attempts to bring the strike before the Commons; but the Labour front bench still regarded the strike as damaging to their standing in the opinion polls. On 31 July 1984 it was opposition day in the Commons – when the opposition choose the subject of the main debate. The miners' strike had now lasted twenty-one weeks, it had dominated the media and there was no break in the miners' solidarity except for those who had worked from the very beginning. Parliament was to adjourn the next day for the summer recess which would last over two and a half months, and by now civil liberties and police methods were causing much public concern. But the motion to which Kinnock spoke in opening the debate was one which condemned the general economic, industrial and employment policies of the Thatcher Government, and Kinnock made only a brief reference to the miners' strike towards the end of his speech. It was an extraordinary performance, given that there was only one issue that everyone in the country was talking about.

Kinnock was leading a Parliamentary Party that was already thoroughly demoralized before the catastrophic electoral defeat of 1983, and he had many political difficulties in addition to the special issues of the coal industry. The problem, however, was that the Labour Party was quite incompetent in dealing with the coal industry and the miners' specific grievances. They had no energy policy, and they were apparently totally ignorant of the economics of the coal industry. During the course of the strike, expert opinion outside the industry, and not in any respect prompted by either the Labour Party or the trade union movement, analysed the National Coal Board accounts and found them seriously deficient and misleading. In the January 1985 issues of *Accountancy* a group of academic accountants from Manchester and Sheffield published a devastating critique of the NCB's accounts and in particular of the guidelines used by which particular mines were declared uneconomic. They took Cortonwood as one of their examples: the pit which had caused the beginning of the strike. Briefly, what the accountants showed was that the NCB's figures of operating costs included items which by no stretch of commercial imagination ought properly to be included. Thus, compensation for surface damage, and for subsidence, were included, and these were costs which would continue whether the pit was kept open or closed. Their conclusion about Cortonwood was that whereas the NCB showed a loss per tonne of £6.20 for 1981–2, the true figure was a positive income per tonne of somewhere between £2.49 and £5.45. And the authors implied – they were cautious in their statements – that the results for 1983–4 would also show a profit. This is what an Oxford economist, Andrew Glyn, had already shown in an earlier study in the autumn of 1984, namely that if certain items were removed from the debit side of the accounts that could not seriously be allocated to operating costs, then the NCB in fact made an operating profit in the year prior to the strike.[2]

A few months after the strike ended another accountant published his analysis of the NCB balance sheets. This was a Mr Emile Woolf, and the interesting thing is that Mr Woolf did not appear to be familiar with the literature just quoted; but it was clear that Mr Woolf was shocked at what he discovered. The NCB accounts, he wrote, were ' a supreme masterpiece in the art of obfuscation. Even if Sherlock Holmes had held a Masters degree in Accounting he would have found his powers of sleuthery stretched to the utmost in finding his way through this particular maze of artfully presented decoys'. Woolf began by referring to the Minister for Energy, Peter Walker's, repeated statement that the taxpayer had subsidized the coal industry by £1,334 million during 1983–4. What everyone naturally assumed from these figures was that the coal industry was making losses of this order; but Woolf showed that a large part of the 'losses' represented payments for the previous contraction of the industry; so that by including these figures in what were presented as 'losses', they helped to make the case for further contraction in the future. As Woolf wrote: 'surely one of the most blatant instances of the proverbial self-fulfilling prophecy ever uttered from an ostensibly authoritative source'. There were other items which were not justifiable, and Woolf summed up:

> If the Secretary of State is really interested in the cause of the £1.3 billion burden on the taxpayer quoted at the beginning of this article the answer is simple. It is made up of the closure, redundancy and early retirement payments already sub-totalled at £634 million; subsidence claims of £245 million; and interest paid to the government of £402 million. By any objective measures the coal industry, based on its audited accounts (as adjusted for distortions), appears to be operationally viable.

And Woolf ended his article in obvious surprise that the National Union of Miners had not used this material and this sort of analysis during the strike: 'Who was advising the Miners?' he asked.[3]

It was a highly pertinent question; to be put also to the Labour Party, the Parliamentary Labour Party, the TUC, as well as to the National Union of Miners. The first answer is that all these bodies were woefully ignorant of the real situation in the mining industry. Their own research departments were pitifully inadequate and while there was some attempt to present the case for the social audit – the economic and social costs of closure as against the costs of keeping pits open – the central criticism of the NCB – that the financial basis upon which closures were decided was wholly inaccurate – was never made in Parliament or outside. The conduct of public relations by the NUM was quite inadequate; that of the TUC non-existent in any meaningful sense; and the political thrust against the NCB and the Government which the Labour front bench in the Commons ought to have made went by default. There was a serious case for the miners' opposition to pit closures which was never made; and public opinion tended to be dominated by the ballot question, and the issue of violence on the picket lines. On the matter of violence, the Labour leadership shamefully ignored the problem, which was not just a matter of the miners, but also of police violence and provocation. There was a great deal of discussion at the time of police violence, and much evidence, but the Labour leadership took the matter as the media presented it; and without the authority, and the persistent statement of the authority, of the Labour leadership, those who protested that the violence was not one-sided were unable to make a significant impact upon public opinion. In the months that followed the ending of the strike, the evidence against the police steadily accumulated, and in no incident has there been more revealing detail than in the case of the supposed riot at Orgreave: a day of physical conflict which probably more than any other single incident convinced large sections of the British public that the miners were guilty of mindless violence. But by mid-August 1985 it had become known that the so-called riot at Orgreave was engineered by the police, and their case hysterically supported by most of the press.[4]

This is not, let it be said again, to suggest that violence was only one-sided, but the miners' violence was the violence of men who were struggling for their jobs, their families and their communities. If the Labour leadership had maintained a principled position on the issue of violence in the strike, and on the very serious questions of civil liberties during the year of the strike, they would have been steadily vindicated by the growing evidence in the months following the ending of the strike. Only fundamentalists believe that politics can be

[149]

conducted, at least with some measure of success, without compromise and adjustment, but unless a radical movement, such as the Labour Party represents, adheres to certain basic obligations to those it purports to represent, it will forfeit their support in the long run. To disappoint gravely your friends, and to give comfort to your enemies, has been a too common practice in the history of Labour in the twentieth century; and in the miners' strike of 1984–5 the mistakes of the past were repeated all too clearly. The response of the rank and file to the miners' strike was remarkable in its moral, material and financial support. In 1926 the largest sum of money donated to the miners' funds had come from the Soviet trade unions; but in 1984–5 by far the largest amounts of help came from within Britain. What was missing was leadership in support of the basic principles the miners were fighting for; and this was never offered. Radical movements must draw material and psychological sustenance from a deep and abiding sense of unity and solidarity. Without that sense of comradeship there will be no self-sacrifice and without the self-sacrifice of individuals and groups there will be no radical movement. The history of the wasted years is eloquent, if bitter, testimony to the inescapable connection between solidarity and sacrifice. There cannot be one without the other.

Notes

2 The nineteenth-century background

1 For industrial relations in the eighteenth century see
  C. R. Dobson, *Masters and Journeymen* (1980). The seminal work for early nineteenth century radicalism is
  Thompson, *The Making of the English Working Class*.
2 Blewett, 'The Franchise in the United Kingdom'.
3 Thompson, *The People's Science*.
4 Thompson, 'The Peculiarities of the English'; and for a
  general elaboration of the previous discussion in the text,
  John Saville, *1848: The British State and the Chartist
  Movement*, Ch.7.
5 The sociology of mining communities has been less
  written about than their working conditions and industrial relations. For a perceptive collection of essays
  relating to the North-east coalfields see Martin Bulmer
  (ed.), *Mining and Social Change* (1978); and for a case
  study of four mining villages, also in the North-east, see

R. Moore, *Pit-Men, Preachers and Politics* (Cambridge, 1974).

6 T. B. Bottomore, introduction to Abercrombie *et al.*, *The Dominant Ideology Thesis*.

7 E. P. Thompson, *William Morris* (London, 1954) and especially Part IV.

3 *The early decades: 1900–26*

1 *The Bitter Cry of Outcast London* (London, 1883) by Andrew Mearns of the Congregational Union was a penny pamphlet which had an extraordinary impact upon public opinion. Henry George (1839–97) was an American whose *Progress and Poverty* was first published in 1879, with its first English edition in 1881. Its intellectual and political influence was considerable. George was not a socialist; his main remedy for poverty was the abolition of land monopoly to be brought about, not by nationalization, but by fiscal policies.

2 For the early history of socialist organizations and parties: H. Pelling, *The Origins of the Labour Party* (1954; 2nd edn, Oxford, 1965); Tsuzuki, *Hyndman and British Socialism*; A. N. McBriar, *Fabian Socialism and English Politics, 1884–1918* (Cambridge, 1962); Howell, *British Workers and the Independent Labour Party*.

3 Quoted by Cole and Postgate, *The Common People* (4th edn, 1949), p. 486.

4 Bell, *Pioneering Days*, p. 57.

5 Simon, *Education and the Labour Movement*, especially Chs. VIII and IX; R. Barker, *Education and Politics*.

6 McKibbin, *The Evolution of the Labour Party*.

7 The 'Curragh incident' of March 1914 came out of the perennial problem of Irish Home Rule. The protestant opposition in Ulster was led by Sir Edward Carson, and some of the officers at the Curragh military base offered their resignations rather than be involved in attempts to 'coerce' Ulster. There is a considerable literature; see A. P. Ryan, *Mutiny at the Curragh* (1950).

8 Bagwell, 'The Triple Industrial Alliance'.

9 There is a growing literature on the analysis of the work process in British industry; for an introduction see some of the essays in Mommsen and Husung, *The Development of Trade Unionism in Great Britain and Germany*.

10 K. Middlemass, *Politics in Industrial Society*; the quotation in the text is taken from the Introduction which provides a helpful summary of his general thesis.

11 The most detailed account is in Arnot, *The Miners: Years of Struggle*, Chs. VI and VII.

12 The literature on the General Strike is voluminous; particularly useful in recent years has been the documentation of local and regional experiences. One of the earliest books is still the best: W. H. Crook, *The General Strike* (Chapel Hill, N. Carolina, 1931). For differing interpretations: Allen Hutt, *The Post-War History of the British Working Class* (1937), a lively Marxist account; Mowat, *Britain between the Wars*, for an excellent liberal version; and Renshaw, *The General Strike*, a good general account with a useful select bibliography.

13 For the record of Labour and imperial questions see Gupta, *Imperialism and the British Labour Movement*.

14 The history of the British Communist Party is still incompletely documented although the literature is growing. A brief critical account is given by H. Pelling, *The British Communist Party. A Historical Profile* (1958); L. J. Macfarlane, *The British Communist Party*; there are two official volumes (1968 and 1969) by James Klugman which take the story up to and including the General Strike; and a short critical account from a *gauchiste* viewpoint: J. Hinton and R. Hyman, *Trade Unions and Revolution: The Industrial Politics of the Early British Communist Party* (1975).

4 The 1930s

1 Mowat, *Britain between the Wars*, Chs. 6–9.

2 Miliband, *Parliamentary Socialism*, Ch. VII. There is a good contemporary account of the period in D. E. McHenry, *The Labour Party in Transition, 1931–38* (1938).

3 The 'social-Fascist' thesis was based on the argument that social democracy (i.e. reformist socialism) was holding the workers back from revolutionary struggle, and was 'objectively' preparing the way for Fascism: hence 'social-Fascism'. Macfarlane, *The British Communist Party*, Chs. 9–12; Branson, *History of the Communist Party of Great Britain*, Chs. 1–3.

4 Branson, *History of the Communist Party*, p. 88 ff.

5 For a general survey of the 1930s, John Saville, 'May Day 1937'.

6 Ellen Wilkinson wrote her own account of the Jarrow march, *The Town that was Murdered*. It was published by the Left Book Club. For Dalton in these years, see B. Pimlott's illuminating biography, published in 1985.

7 For Ernest Bevin in the 1930s, see Bullock, *The Life and Times of Ernest Bevin*, Vol. 1; and for the London busmen's strike, Clegg, *Labour Relations in London Transport*, and K. Fuller, *Radical Aristocrats: London Busworkers from the 1880s to the 1980s* (1985).

8 On Labour's foreign policy see J. F. Naylor, *Labour's International Policy. The Labour Party in the 1930s* (1969), with a good bibliographical essay; and for a Marxist approach different from that presented in the text see Miliband, 'The Challenge of Appeasement', *Parliamentary Socialism*, Ch. VIII.

9 Dalton, *The Fateful Years*, p. 213. For the history of the United Front and the Popular Front movements see Mowat, *Britain between the Wars*, Chs. 10 and 11; Foot, *Aneurin Bevan*, Vol. 1, Chs. 8 and 9; Donoughue and Jones, *Herbert Morrison*, Chs. 16–19. The most comprehensive contemporary statement was by Cole, *The People's Front*; and for a useful collection of essays by Communist writers, Fyrth, *Britain, Fascism and the Popular Front*.

10 Foot, *Bevan*, Vol. 1, p. 307.

11 The social history of the intellectuals and of the intellectual movements of the 1930s is in process of being written. For a very interesting account of five radical scientists see Wersky, *The Visible College*.

5 The Labour Governments: 1945–51

1 Donoughue and Jones, *Herbert Morrison*, p. 304.

2 Skidelsky, *Oswald Mosley*, p. 462.

3 Zilliacus, *I Choose Peace*, p. 75.

4 Barker, 'Some factors in British decision-making over Yugoslavia'; and the extraordinary statement by Sir Fitzroy Maclean in the same volume, pp. 221–8.

5 Quoted by Rosie, *The British in Vietnam*, p. 92.

6 Gowing, *Independence and Deterrence*, p. 406.

7 Dalton, *High Tide and After*, pp. 74–5.

8 Documentation for the statements in the text will be found in Saville, 'The price of alliance'.

9 Sir R. Clarke (ed. Alec Cairncross) *Anglo-American Collaboration in War and Peace, 1942–1949* (Oxford, 1982) p. 152.

10 Harris, *Attlee*, p. 299 for a brief account, largely derived from Dalton's memoirs, of Attlee's differing ideas on defence policy; for a more extended treatment see Bullock, *The Life and Times of Ernest Bevin*, Vol. 3, pp. 242–4 and 348–54.

11 *The Diaries of Sir Alexander Cadogan*, Dilks, p. 776.

12 Acheson, *Present at the Creation*, p. 232.

13 Milward, *The Reconstruction of Western Europe*, especially Chs. I and XIV.

14 The details of American military presence in the United Kingdom are in Campbell, *The Unsinkable Aircraft Carrier*; and for the US constitutional position over the control of the use of nuclear weapons on British soil see Henshaw, 'Whose finger on the button?'

15 Quoted in Bullock, *The Life and Times of Ernest Bevin*, Vol. 3, p. 288.

16 Dalton, *High Tide and After*, p. 147.

17 For general histories of the Attlee administrations see Pelling, *The Labour Governments*, and Morgan, *Labour in Power*. The major biography of Hugh Gaitskell is Williams, *Hugh Gaitskell*.

6 *The wasted years: 1951–79*

1 Gross national product per head, it should be noted, is only a rough guide to a comparative measure of international living standards. Economists are increasingly using purchasing power parities, for which see *National Accounts ESA Aggregates 1960–1985* (Eurostat, Luxembourg, 1987). Purchasing power parities (PPS) also have many problems in their calculation, but on present evidence the UK's position is less unfavourable than it appears from the calculation of GNP, but the fact of a quite sharp relative decline compared with almost all western Europe is not in doubt.

2 Corelli Barnet, about whose work I have certain major reservations, has documented in great detail the inefficiences of British industry in the twentieth century; for which see his latest volume, *The Audit of War*. I would emphasize more than Barnet the harmful affects of the Universities of Oxford and Cambridge upon the whole educational system of the United Kingdom. For a succinct economic analysis of decline, see S. Pollard, *The Wasting of the British Economy* (2nd edn, 1984).

3 See the important article, already quoted, of Henshaw, 'Whose finger on the button?'. Henshaw wrote categorically: 'No American politician I spoke to thinks it [the 1952 agreement between the USA and the UK] gives Britain a veto over the use of bases [in Britain] . . . In the end, it is the American President's constitutional position of Commander-in-Chief of all US forces that means that no formal agreement can take away his ultimate right to use America's weapons in America's national interest.'

4 For an introduction to the literature on the Labour administrations of the 1960s and 1970s: David Coates, *The Labour Party and the Struggle for Socialism* and *Labour in Power?* and for an insider's view, Joe Haines, *The Politics of Power* (revised edn, 1977).

5 Minnion and Bolsover, *The CND Story*.

6 The literature on feminism grows steadily. For an introduction that also has a useful bibliography see Lewis,

Women in England, and for one of the classics of recent writing, *The Rights and Wrongs of Women* (ed. Juliet Mitchell and Ann Oakley, 1976).

7 Hobsbawm's original article, and a number of commentaries upon it, were published in *The Forward March of Labour Halted?* (ed. M. Jacques and F. Mulhern, 1981).

8 Miliband, *The State in Capitalist Society*, a book which gave rise to a vigorous debate in the pages of *New Left Review*, for which see Miliband, *Class Power and State Power* (1983), Part 1. For an example of the socialist writing of the most recent period see Coates *et al.*, *A Socialist Anatomy of Britain*.

9 H. Wainwright and D. Elliott, *The Lucas Plan. A new trade unionism in the making?* (1982).

Epilogue

1 John Saville, 'An open conspiracy: Conservative politics and the miners' strike, 1984–5', *Socialist Register* (1985–6), pp. 295–329.

2 A. Glyn, *The Economic Case against Pit Closures* (NUM, Sheffield, 1984); G. Kerevan and R. Saville, *The Economic Case for Deep-mined Coal in Scotland* (NUM, Scotland, 1985).

3 Emile Woolf, 'Digging holes in the NCB's accounts', *Guardian*, 10 July 1985.

4 There are many accounts of the attitudes and actions of the police during the miners' strike. See, for example, J. Coulter, S. Miller and M. Walker, *A State of Siege: Politics and Policing of the Coalfields: Miners' Strike 1984* (1984); P. Wilsher, D. Macintyre and M. Jones (eds.), with the *Sunday Times* Insight Team, *Strike: Thatcher, Scargill and the Miners* (1985). What really happened at Orgreave, which it is correct to describe as a police 'riot', was revealed in great detail by Gareth Peirce, a solicitor who acted for a group of miner defendants: *Guardian*, 12 August 1985.

Select bibliography

General

There are three easily available sources of bibliographical information:

Smith, H., *The British Labour Movement to 1970; A Bibliography* (foreword by Asa Briggs), London, 1981.

Society for the Study of Labour History, *Bulletins*, twice yearly with consolidated bibliographies in certain individual issues.

Bellamy, J. M. and Saville, J. (eds.), *Dictionary of Labour Biography*, London, 1972. (To date eight volumes have been published with a consolidated name list at the end of each volume and with special bibliographies on selected subjects.)

Books and periodicals

Abercrombie, N., Hill, S. and Turner, B. S., *The Dominant Ideology Thesis*, London, 1980.

[158]

Acheson, D. *Present at the Creation. My Years in the State Department*, London, 1970.

Arnot, R. P., *The Miners: Years of Struggle. A History of the Miners' Federation of Great Britain (from 1910 onwards)*, London, 1953.

Bagwell, P. S. 'The Triple Industrial Alliance, 1913–1922', in Briggs, A. and Saville, J. (eds.), *Essays in Labour History, 1886–1923*, London, 1971.

Barker, E., 'Some factors in decision-making over Yugoslavia, 1941–4', in Auty, P. and Clogg, R., eds., *British Policy towards War-time Resistance in Yugoslavia and Greece*, London, 1975.

Barker, R., *Education and Politics, 1900–1951. A Study of the Labour Party*, Oxford, 1972.

Barnett, C., *The Audit of War*, London, 1986.

Bell, T., *Pioneering Days*, London, 1941.

Blewett, N., 'The Franchise in the United Kingdom, 1885–1914', *Past and Present*, No. 32, December, 1965.

Branson, N., *Britain in the Twenties*, London, 1975.

——, *History of the Communist Party of Great Britain, 1927–1941*, London, 1985.

Bullock, A., *The Life and Times of Ernest Bevin*, Vol. 1; *Trade Union Leader, 1881–1940*, London, 1960; Vol. 2, *Minister of Labour, 1940–1945*, London, 1967; Vol. 3, *Ernest Bevin. Foreign Secretary, 1945–1951*, London, 1983.

Burgess, K., *The Challenge of Labour. Shaping British Society, 1850–1930*, London, 1980.

Campbell, D., *The Unsinkable Aircraft Carrier*, London, 1984; revised edn, 1986.

Citrine, Sir W., *Men and Work*, London, 1964.

Clegg, H. A., *Labour Relations in London Transport*, Oxford, 1950.

Coates, D., *The Labour Party and the Struggle for Socialism*, Cambridge, 1975.

——, *Labour in Power? A Study of the Labour Government, 1974–1979*, London, 1980.

——, Johnston, G. and Bush, R. (eds.), *A Socialist Anatomy of Britain*, Cambridge, 1985.

Cole, G. D., H., *The People's Front*, London, 1937.

——, *British Trade Unionism Today*, London, 1939.

—— and Postgate, R., *The Common People*, London, 1938 (many editions).

Cronin, J. E., *Labour and Society in Britain, 1918–1979*, London, 1984.

Dalton, H., *The Fateful Years, Memoirs, 1931–1945*, London, 1957.
——, *High Tide and After, Memoirs, 1945–1960*, London, 1962.

Dilks, D. (ed.), *The Diaries of Sir Alexander Cadogan*, London, 1971.

Donoughue, B. and Jones, G. W., *Herbert Morrison. Portrait of a Politician*, London, 1973.

Foot, M., *Aneurin Bevan. Vol. 1: 1897–1945*, London, 1962.
——, *Aneurin Bevan. Vol. 2:1945–1960*, London, 1973.

Fyrth, J. (ed.), *Britain, Fascism and the Popular Front*, London, 1985.

Gowing, M., *Independence and Deterrence. Britain and Atomic Energy, 1945–1952*, Vol. 1, *Policy Making*, London, 1974.

Gupta, P. S., *Imperialism and the British Labour Movement, 1914–1964*, Cambridge, 1975.

Harris, K., *Attlee*, London, 1982.

Henshaw, D., 'Whose finger on the button? The President's duty will always be to act in America's interest', *Listener*, 2 June 1983.

Hinton, J., *Labour and Socialism. A History of the British Labour Movement, 1867–1974*, Brighton, 1983.

Howell, D., *British Workers and the Independent Labour Party, 1888–1906*, Manchester, 1983.

Lewis, J., *Women in England, 1870–1950*, London, 1984.

Macfarlane, L. J., *The British Communist Party. Its Origin and Development until 1929*, London, 1966.

McKibbin, R., *The Evolution of the Labour Party, 1910–1924*, Oxford, 1924.

Middlemass, K., *Politics in Industrial Society. The Experience of the British System since 1911*, London, 1979.

Miliband, R., *Parliamentary Socialism. A Study in the Politics of Labour*, London, 1963.
——, *The State in Capitalist Society*, London, 1969.

Milward, A. S, *The Reconstruction of Western Europe, 1945–1951*, London, 1984.

Minnion, J. and Bolsover, P., *The CND Story*, London, 1983.

Mommsen, W. J. and Husung, H. G. (eds.) *The Development of Trade Unionism in Great Britain and Germany, 1880–1914*, London, 1985.

Morgan, K. O., *Labour in Power, 1945–1951*, Oxford, 1984.

Mowat, C. L., *Britain between the Wars*, London, 1955.

Pelling, H., *The Origins of the Labour Party, 1880–1900*, London, 1954 (2nd edn revised, Oxford, 1965).

——, *The Labour Governments, 1945–51*, London, 1984.

Renshaw, P., *The General Strike*, London, 1975.

Rosie, G., *The British in Vietnam. How the Twenty-five Year War Began*, London, 1970.

Saville, J., 'May Day 1937', Briggs, A. and Saville J., (eds.), *Essays in Labour History, 1918–1939*, London, 1977.

——, 'The price of alliance; American bases in Britain', *Socialist Register*, 1987.

——, *1848: The British State and the Chartist Movement*, Cambridge, 1987.

Simon, B., *Education and the Labour Movement, 1870–1920*, London, 1965.

Skidelsky, R., *Oswald Mosley*, London, 1975.

Thompson, E. P., *The Making of the English Working Class*, London, 1963 (2nd edn, 1968).

—— 'The peculiarities of the English', *Socialist Register*, 1965; reprinted with minor changes in *The Poverty of Theory*, London, 1978.

Thompson, N. W., *The People's Science. The Popular Political Economy of Exploitation and Crisis, 1816–1834*, Cambridge, 1984.

Tsuzuki, C., *Hyndman and British Socialism*, Oxford, 1961.

Wersky, G., *The Visible College*, London, 1978.

Wertheimer, E., *Portrait of the Labour Party*, London, 1929.

Wilkinson, E., *The Town that was Murdered*, London, 1939.

Williams, P., *Hugh Gaitskell*, London, 1979 (new paperback edn, 1982).

Zilliacus, K., *I Choose Peace*, Penguin Special, Harmondsworth, 1949.

Index